The Prehistory of Eu

The Prehistory of European Society

V. Gordon Childe

AAKAR

The Prehistory of European Society
V. Gordon Childe

© Aakar Books 2018

First Aakar Edition 2018

ISBN   978-93-5002-529-1

Published by
AAKAR BOOKS
28 E Pocket IV, Mayur Vihar Phase I
Delhi 110 091, India
aakarbooks@gmail.com
www.aakarbooks.com

Printed at
D.K. Fine Art Press, Delhi 110 052

CONTENTS

LIST OF MAPS

PREFACE

THE history of Europe poses two fundamental questions that prehistoric archaeology should be able to answer. Four to five thousand years ago the natives of Europe were on precisely the same level, as far as equipment and economic organization are concerned, as the natives of eastern North America – a very similar environment – were on only 400 years ago and as some native tribes in New Guinea are on today. Why then did they not remain illiterate Stone Age barbarians as the Red Indians and the Papuans did? On an answer to this first question prehistorians are agreed: the proximity of Egypt and Mesopotamia. In the Nile valley and the Tigris-Euphrates delta alone could be created the economic and political organization necessary to get a metallurgical industry started. And there that first step in the 'progress' that has differentiated the Old World from the New was actually taken five thousand years ago. European barbarians profited by that achievement and so left the Stone Age behind.

But this answer at once raises the second question: How could European barbarians outstrip their Oriental masters as they have done? For the essential features of the economy and polity needed to nurture the infant metallurgical industry have persisted in the Orient though the Bronze Age empires of Egypt and Mesopotamia have been replaced by others – the Persian Empire, the Hellenistic monarchies, the Khalifate, the Ottoman Empire, and so on. Incidentally the technological differentiae between the first and the last expressions of the primary pattern – iron, water-wheels, alphabetic writing, pure mathematics, etc. – were inventions introduced or imposed by barbarians, and often European barbarians at that.

In the first edition of my *Dawn of European Civilization* (1925) and in the second edition (1939) I justified the foregoing answer to the first question by a plethora of technical archaeological arguments till the reader might get the impression that European Bronze Age cultures were only degraded and barbarized copies of Oriental civilizations, while in *New Light on the Most Ancient*

Preface

East and in *What Happened in History* I attempted an appreciation
of the magnitude of the Oriental achievement. But in 1940
C.F.C. Hawkes in his *Prehistoric Foundations of Europe* insisted that
the European Bronze Age, far from being just a degradation of
the Oriental, already exhibited progressive and distinctively European innovations, but without explaining to the casual reader
precisely how. In rewriting my *Dawn of European Civilization* in
1955 I thought I did discern both how and why Bronze Age
Europeans could and did diverge from the Oriental standard and
so the answer to the second question. I have presented my conclusions in the sixth edition in technical language buried under a
forbidding accumulation of outlandish culture-names and references to obscure periodicals. Here I have tried to outline the argu-
ment in simpler terms and without abstruse and often inconclusive
archaeological documentation.

Even so, a certain amount of tedious and not very relevant tech-
nicality has crept in. The reader may avoid boredom and still
understand the conclusions by skipping Chapters 4 and 5, except
for pp. 43 and 74–7, and treating the 'megalithic missionaries' and
'warrior herdsmen' in Chapter 8, (i) and (ii), almost as cavalierly.
I have used a certain number of technical terms to save a line of
print by each or just because they sound nice; these are explained
in the glossary-index. Two maps will help readers to locate places
not easily found in an atlas, to understand what I mean by 'Sammland', 'Levant', and other names, and to follow the Amber Route.
Serially numbered notes printed at the end will refer students to
'authorities' where the evidence supposed to justify my statements
is set forth in all its technical details.

In conclusion I am glad to thank my former student and former
colleague, Dr Isobel Smith, for accepting the thankless task of
seeing through the press the typescript of an author in the anti-
podes.

V. GORDON CHILDE

Katoomba, Blue Mountains, Australia
1 June 1957

CHAPTER I

AIMS AND METHODS

THE central object of this book is to show that even in pre-historic times barbarian societies in Europe behaved in a distinctively European way, foreshadowing, however dimly, the contrast with African or Asiatic societies that has become manifest in the last thousand years. Now the most conspicuous and decisive aspect of this contrast has been exhibited in the domains of science and technology. The manifest superiority of European technology has been due to the application of science, though the advance of 'pure' science has just as patently been conditioned by the results of that application. (Wave-mechanics and Relativity could not have been conceived without the copious streams of 'electric current' and the apparatus that applied science, i.e. technology, has made available.) The author indeed contends that the dichotomy between science and technology is historically false. The spiritual ancestors of modern scientists are to be found in preliterate craftsmen more truly than – or at least as truly as – in barbarian magicians or Babylonian priests; the transmutation of metals achieved by nuclear physicists owes more to the successful operations of prehistoric potters and smelters than to the speculations of Alexandrian or Arab alchemists. Granting this assumption, the author hopes to show also why European societies could produce European science. The explanation must of course be sociological not biological. Science, like technology, is the creation of societies not races; its precepts and results are transmitted by social tradition, not 'in the blood'.

The evidence of course is purely archaeological. In

archaeology[1] societies are represented, not by their members' skeletons, but by the durable results of their behaviour – by pots and house-plans, personal ornaments and burial rites, the materials they fetched from afar, and so on. Such remains archaeologists divide and classify into *types*, and, when the same types are repeatedly found together at different sites within a limited region, they are grouped together to represent what we term *cultures*. Pots, house-plans, and the rest can be reduced to abstract types just because they express, not personal idiosyncrasies, but traditional ways of building pots, laying out houses, burying the dead, and decking the person. And types are repeatedly found together just because the traditions they embody are approved and transmitted by a society of persons who can communicate and co-operate. In this sense archaeologists' 'cultures' do really stand for societies.

The cultures here discussed are mostly prehistoric; writing was not an element in the traditional behaviour of the societies to be described, or, if it were, its results have not survived. For this reason the societies are anonymous; we do not know what names they gave themselves and hardly ever what other people called them. So prehistorians assign them conventional, arbitrary, and often outlandish names as labels. Archaeological names are usually those of places where the distinctive types were first identified.

For the same reason archaeological events, the actions of the societies, cannot be dated by kings' reigns or in terms of our era or any other. By purely archaeological means prehistorians can discover a sequence of cultures – the order in which distinct cultures follow one another – in any one naturally defined region. Such culture-periods, often confusingly designated by the same terms as the cultures that define them, provide convenient divisions in the prehistory of Britain, or Crete, or any similar natural province. But such a sequence of cultures gives only a *relative chronology*. It gives no clue as to which archaeological event in Britain is contemporary with which in Crete or elsewhere.

Equally archaeological methods have established a succession of stages in technological or economic progress that follow one another in the same order all over the Old World. Beginning as 'the Three Ages' – the Stone, Bronze, and Iron Ages – they have become Palaeolithic (Lower, Middle, and Upper), Mesolithic, Neolithic, Palaeometallic (Bronze and Iron). But, though everywhere homotaxial (occupying the same position), none of these Stages need be everywhere contemporary: for instance the Neolithic Stage ended before 3000 B.C. in Egypt, in New Zealand only after A.D. 1800! The Ages or Stages are accordingly again only guides to relative chronology.

But of course prehistory, like the rest of history, needs an absolute chronology – a global frame of reference within which archaeological events all over the world can be viewed and compared. Ideally this should be expressed in years marked by the revolutions of our Earth round the Sun. For comparatively recent events such a frame is provided by written records. Written documents containing the names of kings and the lengths of their reigns are available in Egypt from 3000 B.C., in Mesopotamia from about 2500. Under favourable circumstances it is possible, by an exchange of archaeologically dated products, to equate culture periods, for instance in Britain, with dated phases of Egyptian history. But in Europe such synchronisms seldom take us back before 1500, never before 2200 B.C.

On the other hand for very early times – the Pleistocene period of geologists – culture periods can be correlated with geological events affecting the whole Earth – the four major Ice Ages and the consequent changes in sea level.[2] These geological phenomena constitute a global, but very coarse,

The Prehistory of European Society

frame of reference for archaeological events in the Palaeolithic or Old Stone Age. Since 1945 it has been found that
the decay of the radio-active isotope of carbon, C14, may
provide an accurate scale for determining in years the age
of any organic artifact found in an archaeological deposit,
thus dating the deposit itself.[3] The method is still in
its infancy; very few determinations have so far been
published; the results are not always concordant and have
disclosed unforeseen complications. In any case all results
are approximate, with a margin of error of the order of
three centuries either way in some cases. The radio-carbon
dates given in the sequel must be taken as provisional and
approximate; figures like ±350 have been omitted!

Only a fraction of societies' behaviour fossilizes and so
leaves a mark on the archaeological record. In particular
language does not fossilize at all unless committed to writing. So, since we are dealing with preliterate societies, we
cannot apply to them essentially linguistic names like
Celtic, Semitic, or Aryan. Other elements in social behaviour patterns the results of which do not survive can,
rather precariously, be deduced from the results of those
that do. We could not claim to describe societies at all if we
could know nothing of their structure and organization.[4]
Frankly it is impossible from purely archaeological data to
decide whether kinship was reckoned patrilineally or
matrilineally, whether marriage was matrilocal or patri-
local, or even how far cultural uniformity reflected any sort
of political unity. Yet archaeology may give at least hints
on the form of government or on the existence of hierarchical divisions within a society. If a gerontocracy or an
oligarchy would be difficult to recognize thus, single rulers
or leaders should be identifiable by their palaces or their
tombs. Among such indeed it might be possible with the
aid of ethnographic analogies to distinguish two orders. I

should like to suggest a distinction between chief and king. The former, though invested with authority and the rights and duties of leadership and initiative and rewarded with prestige and presents, would be still a member of society – a clansman or tribesman – expected to share with his fellows in most of the fatigues and dangers of economic life and war. A king on the contrary should, like the Egyptian pharaoh, be raised above society, exempt from all manual tasks, and entitled to command. Chiefs interpret custom but are bound by it: kings create laws. Chiefs should be buried in tombs of the same kind as their followers, only bigger and more richly furnished; royal burials should be marked by singular rites and exceptional constructions.

No less important would be division of labour within, or between, communities. The 'natural' division of labour based on sex and age is indeed not likely to be directly documented archaeologically. Still on the analogy of recent societies on a similar technological level, prehistorians generally assume that cooking, spinning, weaving, and the confection of clothing, and also the cultivation of plots without the aid of a plough and the building of domestic pots without the wheel, were women's jobs. Some confirmation of the last assumption may be found in a dactylographic diagnosis as female of the finger prints on a Russian neolithic pot[6] and from the use of rings, normally worn by women, to decorate Iron Age vases in Germany.[6] In social division of labour proper we should distinguish between part-time specialists or experts and full-time specialists or professionals.[7] Ethnographers have familiarized us with 'masters' or 'experts' who, while relying for their living on hunting, fishing, or farming, yet add to their prestige or even their food supply by exercising a craft – flint-knapping, carpentry, or sorcery. In a given community such a man may make arrow-heads or design houses

13

for all the rest, but so long as he grows or catches his own food, he should not be accepted as a professional. The latter must rely for his living entirely on exchanging his craft products for the food produced by his clients. Even if they can be lucky enough to find a flint working place or a potter's workshop, archaeologists can hardly tell whether it was operated by a professional or merely by an expert. On recent analogies they assume that wheel-made pots and cast metal ware were manufactured by full-time professionals. Ethnographic observations indicate that a comparable division of intercommunal specialization is still more hard to determine. Archaeology reveals flint-mines and 'axe-factories' and a wide distribution of their products. The workers were certainly experts. But did they live by bartering their winnings for food produced by farmers, or did they also cultivate crops or breed cattle? In either case did the miners or axe-makers form a distinct community, permanently established round the mine or quarry, or did they resort thither periodically from villages where they normally dwelt with other farmers?[8]

Finally a particularly serious gap in our knowledge of preliterate societies is the total erasure from the record of all direct evidence for socially approved patterns of sexual behaviour. At best we may infer from double graves in which an adult male and an adult female had been buried together that monogamy was normally practised.[9] The inference often drawn of satî (suttee) – i.e. of the slaughter of the wife to accompany her lord – is still more dubious.

The reader should be warned of the hypothetical character of most of archaeologists' conclusions. Here we ask him to accept only the most probable and generally agreed deductions. Even these are at best probable. Simply to avoid tedium I omit the question mark, the 'probably' or 'perhaps', that should qualify most statements.

CHAPTER 2

HUNTERS AND FISHERS IN ICE-AGE EUROPE

EUROPEAN civilization and European societies undoubtedly owe something of their distinctive qualities to the privileged position of the continent between the 35th and 60th parallels, to its long indented coastline conferring on the whole a more moderate and genial climate than is enjoyed by any comparable land mass, and to a wealth of mineral resources. It is needless to recapitulate here what can be learned from any handbook of geography beyond emphasizing certain factors that were peculiarly favourable to cultural development in its earliest stages. Note first the contrast between the Mediterranean Zone with warm dry summers but mild wet winters and the Temperate Zone of deciduous forests and evenly distributed annual rainfall. These contrasted ecological zones demanded divergent adaptations from, and opened up distinct opportunities to, societies separated by no too impassable barriers. The Mediterranean, an enclosed but relatively narrow island-studded sea, like the Baltic and the Irish Sea, was an ideal school for navigators and soon served as a link rather than a bar to the movement of goods and persons and the diffusion of ideas. A comprehensive system of perennial rivers and streams, navigable, albeit with frequent porterages, by light craft, ensured communications throughout the forests of the Temperate Zone. The mountain barrier of the Pyrenees, the Alps, and the Balkans indeed sunders the Mediterranean from the Temperate Zone. But it can be circumvented near both ends, while near its centre a short porterage across the low Brenner Pass leads from the Danube system to the Adige and the Mediterranean.

Map I. Physical map of Europe and the Near East, sh

important regions and settlements referred to in the text.

Finally generous supplies of flint and rock salt, of gold, copper, and above all tin, to which must be added the magic amber of Jutland and Sammland, exerted a potent stimulus to intertribal intercourse even in prehistoric times.

No doubt already during the Pleistocene Ice Ages distinctively European cultures were crystallizing and racial types were becoming genetically adapted to the changing environments. But till the Last Ice Age – the Würm glaciation – we can recognize no peculiarly European culture, still less a European race. Even then the direct contributions of Upper Palaeolithic development to subsequent culture are not at all obvious, while the proportion of native genes carried over by European neolithic societies from the Pleistocene is quite uncertain. Hence for our purposes the Old Stone Age can be dismissed rather summarily.

It must be remembered that while vast ice sheets from the Scottish Highlands and the Scandinavian mountains covered most of Britain north of the Thames and Germany as far as the Saale and glaciers radiated far from the Alps and Pyrenees, beyond the margins of the ice tundras and steppes supported vast herds of large gregarious mammals – mammoths, woolly rhinoceros, bison, wild horse, reindeer. This game, especially the bulky pachyderms, offered an easy and very rewarding prey even to poorly equipped palaeolithic hunters. These created cultures adapted to the pursuit of such game which, however, decayed when the special opportunities that had evoked them passed away. For the Ice Ages were separated by three long warm intervals, termed Interglacials, during which the ice sheets and glaciers melted completely, while each Ice Age was interrupted by one or more Interstadials during which the ice retreated without vanishing altogether.

During the first advance of the Last Ice Age, that is, during Würm I, our continent was populated apparently exclusively by 'men' of Neandertal stock sheltering only in caves and living by hunting, mammoths by preference, with the aid of flint-tipped thrusting spears, heavy missiles, and perhaps simple traps. *Homo neandertalensis* is supposed to be specifically distinct from *Homo sapiens*, the species to which all modern men are assigned. If this be correct, Neandertal men can have made no contribution to the genetic constitution of Europe's population. It would then be hard to see how traditions of the Mousterian culture, with which Neandertalers were equipped for mammoth hunting during Würm I, could have been incorporated in the traditions of later European cultures.

Yet some types of Mousterian equipment and some peculiarities of Mousterian flint technique do seem to re-emerge in later Upper Palaeolithic cultures. But not all Mousterian tools were made by Neandertalers in the strict sense. During the Last Interglacial such tools in Italy and Germany were being made by men who, though definitely Neandertaloid, much more like Neandertalers than you or I, were less highly specialized than their successors during the subsequent Würm Ice Age. It is by no means impossible that such could have communicated with, or perhaps even interbred with, people of modern, *sapiens*, type. It is even conceivable that such an unspecialized Neandertaloid type might have evolved into *Homo sapiens*. Flint industries are known in Palestine[10] that are transitional between the Mousterian and the classical Upper Palaeolithic, and an equally transitional status has been claimed for the 'Audi culture' in France. The latter claim is not now regarded with favour by prehistorians,[11] and moreover men of a type ancestral to *Homo sapiens* were living in England and France before the Last Ice Age.[12]

In any case modern men (of *sapiens* type) appear in force in Europe during the interstadial climatic amelioration that interrupted the Last Ice Age and is labelled Würm I/II. They arrived with a novel culture ready made, or at least with a vastly superior technique of flint-knapping.[13] They had learned to make more efficient flint tools, blades, by a more economical process. With the new tools they could utilize for industrial purposes also bone, antler, and ivory. So they could fashion and arm light missile weapons whose employment augmented almost catastrophically the productivity of hunting and therefore the food-supply, and so permitted and encouraged a rapid expansion of population. Much the same kinds of superior flint implements appear about the same time in North and East Africa and parts of south-western Asia.

In Europe the lucky hunters equipped with the new armoury were able to develop several distinct but rich cultures. Even during the Interstadial the Aurignacians had specialized a variety of bone, antler, and flint tools, including a very rudimentary wood-worker's kit. They pursued cave bears and woodland game more systematically than mammoth and other grass-eaters from the steppes and tundras. Moreover the Aurignacians are the first Europeans known to have taken advantage of the fish with which our rivers were well stocked; Mousterians had conspicuously neglected this valuable source of food. In France the Aurignacians began to develop the magical art that in the subsequent glacial phases culminated in world-famous cave paintings and engravings. They indeed discovered how to represent in two dimensions what they perceived as three-dimensional. The oldest datable applications of this epochal discovery certainly come from Western Europe. That is not to say that the discovery was made in Europe alone and diffused thence, that all pictorial art springs from the childish efforts of the French Aurignacians; but all European palaeolithic and mesolithic pictures probably do.

Ice Age Europe

With the return of the Ice Age, as Würm II, woodlands gave place once more to steppes or tundras even in Western Europe. There and in Central Europe, the Ukraine, and South Russia too the Gravettian culture emerges as an adjustment to glacial conditions. The Gravettians pursued by preference gregarious game – mammoth, bison, wild horse – on steppes where every summer bitter winds blowing off the ice were depositing a layer of dust to form the younger löss. They tipped their missiles with points of flint instead of bone. The Gravettians had learned to construct artificial shelters[14] without which the pursuit of mammoth on the open steppe would have been impossible. The huts were dug out in the löss to a depth of a couple of feet, roofed with hides supported on a frame of tusks or saplings, and half buried in heaped-up earth to exclude the icy blasts. Gravettians too produced works of art – not of course just for art's sake alone but also for magico-religious ends. Best known are little figures of women, carved out of mammoth ivory or soft stone or even moulded in clay and ash. The sexual characters are always emphasized while the faces are literally featureless. (On only two out of over sixty statuettes have any facial features been indicated.) The figures were supposedly used in some ritual to promote the fertility of nature. Inevitably the ceremonies and the beliefs that inspired them, or were generated by them, remain unknown. But similar female figurines were manufactured by nearly all early peasant societies in South-Western Asia and South-Eastern Europe. So were little models of animals, but peasants modelled bulls and cows, Gravettians mammoths and other game.

During the same glacial phase the development of Upper Palaeolithic blade traditions seems interrupted by the spread of the celebrated 'Solutrean culture'. This culture should strictly be termed an industry; it is nothing more than a new method of thinning flint flakes and the superior spear- and missile-tips made by its application. Since the types thus produced are not everywhere identical and are associated with other different types in each province, prehistorians are today inclined to regard this 'culture' or industry rather as a cycle of cultures, confining the term Solutrean to West European assemblages and designating Szeletian[15] their analogues in Central Europe. A further group may be recognized in Eastern Europe from the Don to the Kuban,[16] while the North African Aterian and the East African Still Bay cultures exhibit 'Solutrean' forms and techniques, but have never been called Solutrean. The innovations on the common Upper Palaeolithic blade tradition in all these assemblages include a revival of some Mousterian types and techniques. All might therefore have arisen independently at several places and denote a fusion of Mousterian traditions with local Upper Palaeolithic ones. Yet in South Russia the innovations in question are detectable in the mild Interstadial, whereas further west they do not appear before the succeeding cold Würm II phase. At the same time both in South Russia and in Spain and, though less explicitly, in North Africa too some of the products look like arrow-heads. If appearances be not deceptive, they would then be the first indications of the invention of a bow. The likelihood of some sort of contact between the various societies that adopted 'Solutrean' techniques certainly cannot be ruled out. In particular mutual agreements between Spain and North Africa appear so striking that direct communications across the Mediterranean and therefore some sort of boat seem fair deductions.

Be that as it may, in Western and Central Europe the 'Solutrean' seems a brief episode that exercised no recognizable influence on subsequent developments. In Eastern Europe on the contrary Solutrean techniques were applied at times to the later East Gravettian (Kostienki)[16] flint-work and survived locally even in the Mesolithic Swiderian industry to which we return on p. 26.

During the long and discontinuous retreat of the ice sheets and glaciers, the successful pursuit of reindeer and bison herds and the systematic exploitation of salmon runs in North Spain, France, South Germany, and Bohemia, supported what seems the richest and most brilliant culture ever created by food-gatherers in any part of the world – the Magdalenian. Its claim to this unique distinction rests primarily on the high quality of the naturalistic art expressed in engravings and paintings in the remote recesses of dark and inaccessible caverns, in bas-reliefs in shallow rock-shelters, and in innumerable carvings and engravings in mammoth ivory, bone, and antler, on pebbles and even on lumps of amber and ochre. This art was of course rooted in the older Aurignacian and Gravettian, but culminates in the Magdalenian. It appeals to contemporary Europeans in virtue of its direct naturalism and immediacy. Animals are represented with marvellous sympathy and accuracy as they were seen, undistorted by conceptual thought. Each picture or sculpture is the portrait of an individual beast. The rare representations of the human form[17] on the contrary appear to us as grotesque caricatures – a phenomenon not due to any incompetence of Magdalenian artists, but to a peculiarity of the perceptual equipment of all savages and barbarians. Nothing deserving the title of human portraiture is older than the Narmer palette, than the Urban Revolution!

Magdalenian art and the magic rituals it served were by-products of a material culture beautifully adapted to the peculiarly propitious circumstances of late glacial Europe. With the end of the Ice Age that culture collapsed, and with it the art and ceremonial it had supported vanished leaving no trace. Items of Magdalenian hunting equipment and fishing tackle no doubt survived; no comparable survival of artistic or ceremonial traditions is detectable. In the present context that fact justifies the cursory treatment of a glorious episode.

In Eastern Spain and Sicily[18] and in North Africa[19] too hunters painted or engraved pictures on rocks. These also may be inspired by the Aurignacian tradition, but in style they diverge widely from the Magdalenian. The East Spanish paintings are lively impressionistic scenes, not indeed conventionalized symbols, but still somewhat conceptualized. In general style and sometimes even in points of detail they are absurdly like some paintings from round the Sahara and even the Bushman paintings of Rhodesia. The series may begin during the Spanish Gravettian or Solutrean phase. It certainly went on till herdsmen with tame sheep had reached the Peninsula.[20] North African artists too depicted herdsmen as well as hunters. In the rest of Europe Gravettian traditions, occasionally modified by 'Solutrean', persisted during the late glacial period without producing any significant modification as far as archaeologists can tell. We may just mention a camp of mammoth-hunters, buried in the löss at Mezin in the Ukraine, because of the unusual decorative art illustrated there. Ivory bracelets and other small articles were engraved all over with continuous maeanders used as a repetition pattern, i.e. repeated in all directions so as to blanket the whole surface. The motive thus employed, though easily produced in basketry, is surprisingly rare in ancient art, but was systematically used by early neolithic farmers precisely on the South-East European löss lands.

At last the long Ice Age drew to its close. The glaciers retreated towards the high mountains; the vast Scandinavian and Scottish ice sheets gradually melted and shrank.

Forest trees invaded the steppes and tundras of what was henceforth to be Temperate Europe. The fauna changed with the climate and vegetation. The mammoth was already extinct; the reindeer followed the ice margins northward. The herds of gregarious herbivores that had grazed on the steppes were replaced by more solitary game – red deer, roe deer, wild oxen, wild boars – the pursuit of which required more arduous tactics and a new equipment. That spelt the end of the cultures that had brought prosperity to Upper Palaeolithic hunters. Adaptations to the novel and really sterner conditions are represented by so-called mesolithic cultures.[21] All are equally based on hunting, fishing, and collecting, although in each the huntsmen were assisted by more or less domesticated dogs.

A few descendants of the Magdalenians, termed Azilians, lingered on in France, sheltering in caves and securing a meagre subsistence by collecting wild food, fishing, and catching small game. They do not seem to have possessed a bow any more than the Magdalenians.

Interspersed among the Azilians, but ranging much further – all around the Western Mediterranean, northward to Britain and Northern Europe and again on the steppe hinterland of the Black Sea – lived bands of archers who encamped generally on sandy tracts in the forests or on windswept coasts. They are known almost exclusively from the 'pigmy flints' or 'geometric microliths' with which they armed their darts and arrows. (Their microliths are qualified as 'geometric' because many of these minute blades have been neatly trimmed to regular geometric shapes – triangles, trapezes, crescents.) All these archers used to be lumped together under the blanket title 'Tardenoisian', but closer study and statistical analyses have revealed the shadowy outlines of several distinct cultures – an Epigravettian in the Iberian Peninsula, a Grimaldian in

Italy, a Sauveterrian in France and Britain have so far been provisionally identified. Curiously similar microlithic industries occur far beyond the frontiers of Europe – even in India and Australia, but above all in Africa. These far-flung geometric industries, peculiar though they seem, can hardly all be derived from a single tradition. Indeed in Europe later Gravettian flint-workers showed an inclination to reduce their blades to pigmy size and to give them geometrical outlines, particularly round the Mediterranean but also in central France.[22] On the other hand West European microlithic assemblages seem to resemble so closely the North African Capsian that an immigration of African hunters has been assumed. African connexions must certainly be admitted for the Spanish Epigravettians if these painted the pictures mentioned on p. 24, albeit without prejudice to the question of their direction.

Finally in the forest zone of Eastern Europe roamed other archers – Swiderians – whose arrow-armament, though microlithic, was not geometric. The traditions of their flint-work which alone are known might well be traced back to the East Gravettian of Kostienki (p. 21).

Really very little is known of these early holocene hunters. Geometric microliths have been found in caves both in Western Europe and the Crimea, in irregular hut-foundations in Western Europe, and in midden heaps along the Atlantic coasts. Certain Sauveterrian burials in a Ligurian cave and on islets off the coast of Brittany seem to indicate differences of rank within the band, and there is one unambiguous case of homicide. From the interment together in the Crimea of a mature man and a female half his age might be inferred a patriarchal family and the practice of satî. Boats of some sort were available for short voyages. Presumably all these archers hunted, fished, collected snails, berries, and other wild food. But some may have kept a few sheep or goats whose milk or blood might have supplemented the products of hunting and collecting; a very few stray bones of these animals have been found with Sauveterrian relics far beyond their natural habitat even in Brittany and Devon. So some Sauveterrian food-gatherers may rank as food-producers too. To that extent some mesolithic cultures might be termed neolithic too. But none of the communities so far mentioned is known to have devised any equipment for dealing effectively with the most prominent item in the post-glacial European environment – the timber of the temperate forests. That was developed among descendants of palaeolithic Europeans who had spread northwards, perhaps in the wake of the reindeer herds, to colonize lands newly freed from ice.

The retreating ice sheets had laid bare a wide stretch of marsh and tundra on the North European plain round the Baltic depression and extended westward to England by 'Northsealand'; for the ocean waters had not yet inundated the North Sea basin so that dry land, interrupted by a swollen Thames and Rhine and many channels from the shrinking Scandinavian ice sheet, still united England with the Continent. What was happening in Northsealand can only be guessed, since all remains of human activity are buried in mud and silt below that sea. Bands of reindeer-hunters, we know, had penetrated as far north as Hamburg [23] while the edge of the ice sheet still ran across Denmark and north-east Germany. They encamped on the tundra only in summer and autumn for seasonal hunting and fowling, retiring south to winter among the advancing woods. These pioneers, termed Hamburgians, combined some Magdalenian traditions with others derived from Central or Eastern Europe. So, unlike the Magdalenians, they used some kind of bow. Later, when the whole Continent was ice-free, they were followed by other bands who at first encamped in the north only in summer, but subsequently were able to winter as far north as Jutland.

Eventually when birch woods and a vanguard of pines had colonized the tundras we find societies beginning to develop a distinctive and highly efficient equipment for the exploitation of the rich natural resources of the plain that then extended from the Pennines to the Urals; for Northsealand had not yet been submerged and land bridges across the Belts and the Sound left the Baltic a brackish lake – the Ancylus Lake of geologists. The development of the appropriate culture can be followed through three successive phases that are defined by changes of climate reflected in the local vegetation. These climatic phases can in turn be provisionally dated by radio-carbon estimates.

During the first or Pre-Boreal phase the climate of eastern England as well as of Denmark and southern Scandinavia was still very cool and continental. A lakeside encampment of four households at Star Carr near Scarborough (Yorkshire)[24] reveals already the essential outlines of the Maglemose culture-cycle that in its mature shape is so well known in the succeeding Boreal phase – arrows armed with geometric microliths for hunting, antler-pronged leisters for spearing fish, heavy flint adze-blades, sharpened ingeniously by the so-called *tranchet* blow for wood-chopping.

A thousand years later in the Boreal phase the climate had grown milder – indeed the mean annual temperature was higher than today, though the winters in Denmark, southern Sweden, and Britain were more severe and snowy. Dense coniferous forests extended from the Pennines to the Urals to join up there with the Siberian pine woods to form a continuous belt of *taiga* – to use a familiar Russian term – girdling Europe from the Atlantic to the

Pacific and extending across North America to meet the Atlantic again. But during the latter half of the genial Boreal phase oaks with elms, limes, and other trees that usually accompany them began to mingle with the pines till in the end mixed oak woods became the dominant vegetation of England and Denmark. No North Sea as yet interrupted the continuity of the forest. Northsealand was doubtless largely fen, but beyond it the only gaps in the endless forest were the Ancylus Lake in the Baltic depression and a myriad smaller lakes, meres, marshes, and sluggish streams. Their waters were well stocked with fish, while their banks were frequented by game and innumerable birds. Combined with wild berries and nuts the fish, fowl, and game provided a generous diet for an expanding population of hunter-fishers. The latter are best known from the refuse dropped at temporary summer camps on the edges of meres that have since become covered with preservative peat and so are aptly termed Maglemoseans after Maglemose – the Big Moss – near Mullerup in Zealand where a seasonal camp was first excavated.

The Maglemoseans had discovered all the main resources useful to man in Northern Europe and had devised or inherited an equipment for their exploitation so ingenious that much of it survives unaltered to the present day. Hunters and fowlers were armed with bows, some reinforced with sinews, and a variety of arrows specialized for the slaughter of particular game; arrows with conical tips of wood or bone were presumably used, as they still are, for killing fur-bearing animals with minimum damage to pelts. Fish were caught with hook and line and in nets or ingenious wicker traps or weels, while large species were speared with bone-pronged leisters.[25] For tree-felling or wood-working the Maglemoseans possessed an efficient carpenters' kit of adzes, chisels, and gouges of flint edged by a *tranchet* blow, or of fine-grained stone sharpened by grinding, supplemented by chisels and wedges of bone and antler. They had even devised a way of mounting a flint blade in a transversely perforated section of antler beam to produce the effect of a modern iron axe- or adze-head. (The reader must remember that stone and even copper axe-heads were normally stuck into the handle instead of being fitted on to it with the aid of a hole or eyelet through the head.)

Thanks to these primary tools the Maglemoseans could build transport devices. Runners survive to represent sledges,[26] probably drawn by men, but capable of development into dog-sledges such as were actually used quite early in post-Atlantic times. On water, paddles, preserved in the peat, must have been used to propel canoes of skin or birch-bark that have perished. Finally the Maglemoseans had learned how to make a good adhesive from birch bark by the application of heat[25] – the oldest artificial substance to be made by man at least in Europe. Yet the Maglemoseans must have led a nomadic existence, and certainly shifted their habitations seasonally from winter quarters to summer camps. Only the latter are known; they are represented by a couple of flimsy huts of birch bark and hides. Still a more sedentary version of the Maglemosean culture may have been developing on the sea coasts. Any settlements on the shores of Northsealand are of course now under water, but collections of flint implements from high strand lines in Norway may belong to such a population already pursuing the marine mammals of the Arctic Ocean.

During the millennium 6000 to 5000 B.C. this Maglemose culture, although differentiated into several local variants, is recognizable all over the former plain from Southern Britain to Finland and the East Baltic republics. Further east most Maglemose types recur in the coniferous zone of

Northern Russia as far as the Urals; many reappear still further east all through the taiga belt of Northern Eurasia and North America. But none has been found even in North Russia in contexts dated to the Boreal phase by pollen analysis or radio-carbon, and many indubitably remained current much later; not a few are still in use today. Hence the distribution of the Maglemose culture east of the Baltic before 4000 B.C. remains dubious. What is certain is how much of the folk culture of Northern Eurasia[25] is directly inherited from the Maglemosean of that epoch; birch pitch, the ingenious wicker fish-traps, nets secured with the same fast, but by no means self-evident, knots, leisters – though iron has replaced bone – to mention only a few outstanding examples are still employed among the coniferous forests today. That means that both the techniques for their manufacture and prescriptions for their use have been handed down among local populations by oral tradition for a full 8,000 years over more than 300 generations. Other devices such as conical-headed arrows, sledge-runners, still employed by circumpolar peoples, are just as directly derived from Maglemosean models, though slightly more modified. Here we have a striking demonstration both of the excellence of the Maglemoseans' adaptation to their environment and of the debt we owe to preliterate European savages!

Towards 4000 B.C. a general rise in Ocean levels finally separated Great Britain from the Continent, Scandinavia from Denmark and North Germany. As a result the climate of Northern Europe became moister, but no colder, than in the Boreal phase; Denmark and Southern Sweden enjoyed, or endured, an Atlantic climate, comparable to that of Brittany or Cornwall today, so that the term Atlantic is employed, rather confusingly, to designate this phase throughout Northern Europe. In response to the heavier and more frequent rainfall oak woods spread further than before and were now interspersed with beeches. The deciduous forests interposed more serious obstacles to communications than the Boreal pine woods, while the new North Sea and Channel put an end to dry-land traffic between England and the Continent. At the same time the North Sea and the Litorina Sea that now filled the Baltic depression offered fresh opportunities to hunters and fishers.

So the relatively homogeneous Maglemosean culture-cycle broke up into a multiplicity of local cultures, each adapted to the peculiarities of the local environment. None is so well known as the Maglemosean, since few encampments were located where a subsequent growth of peat ensured the preservation of wood, bone, and other organic materials. Most have to be inferred from collections of far from distinctive stone implements. It will suffice to mention here the Ertebølle culture of Denmark, derived probably from the hypothetical coastal version of the Maglemosean (p. 30) and certainly adapted to take advantage of the food supplies offered by the Litorina Sea. It was the creation of strand-loopers whose encampments are represented by the Kitchen Middens – huge heaps of shells along that Sea's ancient shore. The reliable supplies of food offered by the salt waters and the great oyster banks of the Sound, the Belts, and the Kattegat allowed of more permanent settlements occupied all the year round. In them are found the oldest pottery vessels known from Northern Europe. Perhaps the sedentary hunter-fishers themselves had discovered how by heat to effect the chemical change that converts plastic clay into solid water-tight vessels. But they may have been taught this art by immigrant farmers, who certainly introduced cereals and sheep and goats – plants and animals quite alien to the North European flora and fauna. By 4000 B.C. at latest (according to radio-carbon estimates) Danubian peasants had spread as far north as Magdeburg on the Elbe. The subsequent prehistory of European societies save in the taiga zone was conditioned by the new food-producing economy based on cultivation and stock-breeding. However much this was adopted by aboriginal stocks, however much its adaptation was accomplished in Europe, however far the social organization within which it worked was elaborated in that continent, the basis of the new way of life – the actual cereals and the domestic stock – were introduced from outside.

CHAPTER 3

THE NEOLITHIC REVOLUTION IN THE ANCIENT EAST

PLANT-CULTIVATION and stock-breeding – in a word, food-production – constituted an epoch-making innovation. It is rightly taken to mark in archaeology the beginning of a new age – the Neolithic or New Stone Age – or in socio-economic terms the boundary between Savagery and Barbarism.[27] Throughout the several hundred millennia of the Old Stone Age all human societies all over the world remained parasitic, depending entirely for their food on what natural processes happened to supply. Neolithic societies began deliberately co-operating with nature to increase the productivity of edible plants and to protect and foster the multiplication of animals that yield food as meat, blood, or milk.

In Europe this new productive economy still seems to appear fully-fledged. It is represented by farmers who cultivate cereals, leguminous plants, and flax, and breed sheep, goats, cattle, and pigs, who live in commodious well-built houses, grouped in villages, and who are equipped with efficient axes or adzes, edged by polishing, and have mastered the arts of converting clay into pottery and of spinning and weaving. Neolithic villages are more numerous and more populous than the camps of palaeolithic – or mesolithic – hunters and fishers. The human population must have increased, and such an increase was only to be expected. Comparative demography shows that the opening up of fresh food-supplies is normally followed by a multiplication of consumers. Were the statistical data available, the European population graph would certainly show at the beginning of the New Stone Age a sharp kink and upward bend comparable to what ensued upon the Industrial Revolution in England. That analogy is my excuse for speaking of a 'Neolithic Revolution'.[28] The term does not imply a single catastrophic change. The Industrial Revolution itself was only the culmination of a gradual process, begun centuries earlier. The prelude to the Neolithic Revolution must have been much longer, and it is less easy to decide what precisely should be termed its culmination.

The preparatory stages are not to be expected in Europe. Our first farmers cultivated wheats and barleys – improved and selected forms of wild annual grasses.[29] The wild ancestor of only one species of wheat grew spontaneously on European soil, and that only in the Southern Balkans. But this 'one-corn' wheat is a very poor crop, and was normally grown only in conjunction with the much superior emmer wheat or some mutation product of the latter. The wild ancestor of emmer grows in nature from Iran to Palestine and Southern Turkey. In the latter region its habitat overlaps with that of wild one-corn. Wild barley is native to the same province. In other words the cereals on which neolithic farming was based must have been introduced from South-west Asia. The same may be asserted of sheep and goats, albeit with less confidence.[30] As the essential constituents of our Neolithic economy were not indigenous to Europe, the Neolithic Revolution did not happen there. Evidence for the preliminary stage of incipient food-production should on *a priori* grounds be expected in South-west Asia and at a date not later than the end of the European Ice Age. Since 1945 farming villages have there been found that in radio-carbon age are contemporary with the oldest mesolithic camp of hunter-fishers in Northern Europe (at Star Carr[24]): Jericho 1, like the Pre-Boreal climatic phase, began not later than 7000 B.C.[31]

A perennial spring made the site of Jericho[32] an oasis in the virtual desert of the Rift Valley beyond the Jordan. Its water will irrigate a fertile soil to provide regular harvests and pasture for stock through the dry season. Some nine thousand years ago by exploiting these opportunities a community had grown large enough to defend a space, about six acres in area, with a rock-cut ditch 27 feet wide and 8 feet deep, and a stone-built rampart inside it, and to erect at least one massive stone tower, 35 feet in diameter and over 25 feet high. So the villagers were numerous enough to accomplish this constructional feat with very crude stone tools, while the region was already so populous as to make this stupendous labour seem necessary! In fact after several reconstructions the site was deserted for a while, to be then re-occupied by a different but also vigorous community. Under the shelter of a new wall the newcomers built themselves commodious houses of mud brick and stone before 6000 B.C., about the time Maglemoseans were establishing summer camps in Denmark during the North European Boreal phase.

Both the societies that successively occupied Jericho, in addition to hunting and collecting, must have cultivated cereals and bred sheep and goats for food. Neither is believed to have kept cows. Moreover, in contrast to later neolithic peasants, neither used ground stone axes or made pottery. They illustrate what is now termed a pre-pottery neolithic stage. Jericho was certainly not unique, but no other settlement of comparable age has been discovered, or rather none has been dated so early by radio-carbon. The next oldest known village, radio-carbon-dated to only 4750 B.C., but still pre-pottery neolithic, is Jarmo in Kurdistan.[33] Here the villagers were indubitably cultivating emmer and barley; the grains, which actually survive,[29] though nearer to wild cereals than any other cultivated species so far examined, already exhibit unmistakable signs of domestication and imply a considerable previous history as cultivated plants. The villagers also possessed most of the equipment, material and ideological, used by later neo-lithic farmers – querns or rubbers to reduce grain to flour, domed clay ovens in which to bake flour into bread, adzes or axes edged by grinding, figurines of women modelled in unbaked clay, clay stamps capable of multiplying geo-metric motives by impression and in one instance bearing a spiral design. They could build houses of mud brick, as could the villagers of Jericho II, and fashion delicate vessels out of stone, but they made no pots till the very latest phase of the village. A pre-pottery neolithic stage is repre-sented also at Khirokitia in Cyprus, in the Belt Cave, south of the Caspian,[34] and at Kili Gul Mohammed in Balu-chistan.[35] But the radio-carbon age of the last-named site is not more than 3500 B.C.! A pre-pottery neolithic is no more universally older than the more familiar variant than is food-gathering everywhere older than food-producing.

Next in order of radio-carbon age are neolithic encamp-ments on the edge of a lake, now dry, in the Fayum depres-sion west of the Nile, thus dated 4440–4150 B.C.[36] But they are not necessarily older than the Levantine neolithic of Mersin in Cilicia, Byblos on the Phoenician coast and the Orontes basin or the Hassunan of the Euphrates-Tigris basin, nor for that matter than Sialk I[36] on the Iranian plateau and Anau I on the northern slopes of the Kopet-dagh in Turkmenia. In all these provinces pottery was now made. Its variations from region to region, together with divergent preferences for adzes or axes, for slings or bows-and-arrows and so on suffice to distinguish quite a number of cultures or societies.

So before 4000 B.C. anonymous peoples had domesticated and improved local annual grasses till they became
wheats and barleys, and had tamed sheep, goats, oxen, and
swine; they had devised equipment for the harvesting,
storage, and processing of crops. They had learned how to
build vessels out of clay and convert them into pots by
firing. All must have established social institutions to
ensure co-operation at least in village communities. Finally
they had elaborated ideologies and rituals that cemented
the community's cohesion and lubricated personal contacts. The institutions and the ideologies escape our ken,
but a part of the rituals has fossilized. A prominent part
therein was played by female figurines, modelled in clay
or carved in ivory, bone, or stone, that are found alike in
Egypt and Asia. They are held to represent a Mother Goddess, a personification at once of Earth from whose womb
the harvest and the fresh grass spring and of Woman as the
source of life. They may at the same time reflect at least an
'economic matriarchy'. The plough being still unattested,
it is assumed that the tillage of garden plots and the tendance
of the crop fell to the women of the community.[4] As the
chief providers of the community's food, the females could
therefore claim economic influence, though not necessarily more successfully than agricultural labourers in
1935!

Several elements, characterizing these Oriental neolithic
cultures, reappear in Europe. The emmer and barley at
least must have been carried thither by actual immigrant
cultivators. The sheep and goats were presumably driven in
by shepherds and neatherds. The immigrants must have
carried with them the appropriate techniques of husbandry,
but not of course a complete rural economy: for the
European environment was too unlike that of the Near
East. Actually the rural economies of early Oriental farm-

ing are hardly known, but were certainly not uniform. Jericho and Sialk must have relied on irrigation to water their crops. The Levantine and Hassunan sites as well as Jarmo all lie in a zone where the rainfall, though small, still suffices in normal years to guarantee a harvest. So dry cultivation was presumably the rule. But till some regular system of rotation has been worked out, dry cultivation imposes a degree of nomadism on the cultivators.[28] The same plot will not yield a decent crop for more than a couple of years; thereafter fresh virgin soil must be opened up. When all the conveniently accessible land has been thus exhausted, the whole community must shift bag and baggage to a new tract of virgin soil. Food-producers, practising this system of shifting cultivation, are compulsorily mobile, indeed more mobile than some favourably situated food-gatherers. The incessant quest for virgin soil combined with the need to find fresh land for farmers' younger children must be the reason for the early spread of neolithic culture or rather of wheat and barley, sheep and goats. Since farmers had reached the Middle Elbe by 4000 B.C. (p. 33) the expansion towards Europe must have begun during the obscure period of incipient food-production, the pre-pottery neolithic. No European neolithic culture reproduces wholly the lineaments of any one of the neolithic cultures that crystallized out after 4500 B.C. in the Near East.

The distinctive traditions of these cultures are conveniently expressed for archaeologists in pottery. But even as defined in this sensitive medium the earlier neolithic cultures of North-east Africa and South-west Asia display extraordinary uniformity over quite wide areas. The banks of the Nile from above the First Cataract down almost to the Delta in the Predynastic Period[36] were lined with farming villages illustrating the Badarian culture which

39

grows into the equally uniform Amratian but is sprung from the same root as the Fayum neolithic. The Predynastic peasants relied on natural irrigation by the Nile's annual flood and everywhere exhibit the same behaviour patterns in hunting and fishing tackle, burial rites and toilet articles as much as in pottery. In Hither Asia[36] the Hassuna culture probably, its successors the Halafian and 'Ubaid certainly, are no less homogeneous from the Iranian foothills east of the Tigris to the Levant coasts and Cilicia. But in the latter regions Halaf and 'Ubaid replace an older Levantine neolithic. These four major cycles do not of course exhaust the list of distinguishable neolithic cultures, and in the sequel their local variants themselves tend to turn into separate cultures. Only a few common features need be mentioned here.

Even in the pre-pottery neolithic village of Jericho stood a large building plausibly identified as a shrine. In Halafian settlements there were indubitable sanctuaries which can be watched growing in succeeding culture-periods into the monumental temples of the historical epoch. In other words a temple, albeit rudimentary, formed the nucleus of early villages in Hither Asia; it implies a deity and perhaps the germ of a professional priesthood.

Predynastic Egyptian (Amratian), Halafian and Levantine villages, and even Jericho and Jarmo were continuously occupied over many generations. In all these cultures, therefore, shifting cultivation had been abandoned. Now the Amratians doubtless relied on natural irrigation by the Nile's flood both to water their crops and to restore fertility to their exhausted fields. Halafian farmers too spread into Lower Mesopotamia (Babylonia) and there could likewise rely upon the waters of the Tigris and Euphrates. But in the rest of Hither Asia where dry cultivation is believed to have been the rule, the sedentary villagers must have devised and practised systematic alternation between tillage and pasture. Moreover by 3000 B.C. all peasants in the area had yoked oxen to the plough and begun to cultivate fields therewith instead of just hoeing plots. But just how early this revolution in rural economy had taken place is still unknown.

Very early in the Oriental neolithic some sort of irregular and rudimentary trade brought to the settled villagers luxury articles from remote places – bright pebbles from the deserts whose aesthetic appeal was at least reinforced by supposed magical virtues, and equally magical shells – to the Fayum from the Mediterranean and the Red Sea, to Halafian Syria from the Persian Gulf. Even industrially useful substances like obsidian were likewise widely distributed. Small articles of copper too had been brought to Badarian and Halafian villages. The first are probably made of native copper; for copper sometimes occurs native in the metallic state as gold does. By the 'Ubaid phase in Mesopotamia and by the Gerzean phase in Egypt the secrets of extracting copper from its ores by the chemical process of reduction – i.e. smelting, and of shaping it by fusion and casting in a mould, were known. (Asiatic potters' kilns, derived ultimately from bread ovens, may have supplied the requisite temperature.) However, metal could not really begin to replace stone, bone, and wood as an industrial material till a veritable economic revolution made it profitable to organize a regular system for the distribution of this rather scarce element. Only thereafter is it useful to introduce a fresh term to designate a new archaeological stage. This should be Palaeometallic, but Bronze Age has been traditionally but incorrectly used by prehistorians since 1836. In practice copper was nowhere regularly, and even then not universally, alloyed with tin to form bronze for a thousand years after the Palaeometallic Stage was well established in Egypt, Mesopotamia, and the Levant. (The term Chalcolithic or even Copper Age is often applied to cultures like the Badarian, Amratian, or Halafian, the remains from which include stray objects of copper. But it is more profitable to postpone the introduction of a new section heading in the archaeological record till the technical advances imply also comprehensive economic and sociological changes.)

CHAPTER 4

THE COLONIZATION OF EUROPE
BY FARMERS

THE bases of the new neolithic way of life were doubtless introduced into Europe by bodies of immigrant cultivators and herdsmen. But the migrants who brought hither cereals and domestic stock cannot be traced in the archaeological record. They certainly have left no trail of Oriental pots or other Near Eastern types to mark their route and indicate their starting-points. They may well have been in the pre-pottery neolithic stage; in Western Europe some 'mesolithic' microliths may mark their trail (p. 26). The phase of immigration remains a postulate. An ensuing phase of colonization is, however, represented by clearly recognizable cultures, by societies with distinct traditions in pottery, architecture, and industrial equipment. These may of course have already incorporated mesolithic aboriginals or even have been composed of such native European food-gatherers as had appropriated the immigrants' seeds and stock. But it is them we see actually occupying European soil, clearing the continuous virgin forests and opening up routes for intercourse or tribal movement. And they began adapting a rural economy appropriate to drier and warmer climes to the environments of Mediterranean and Temperate Europe.

These pioneer colonists are represented by three or four cultures:[37] a Starčevo culture in the Balkan Peninsula and round the Carpathians; a cognate Cardial culture on the coasts and islands of the central and western Mediterranean; the Danubian culture of the löss lands of Central Europe; and a more hypothetical Western culture in the Iberian

43

Peninsula and Atlantic Europe. All display a remarkable uniformity throughout the vast areas they came to occupy. In any one of such huge provinces all settlements can hardly have been contemporary and strict chronological parallelism between the several cultures is no more likely. If all be here assigned to an 'Early Neolithic', this term denotes the stage of colonization rather than a definite period of sidereal time. In so far as temporal limits can be assigned to it, they must be very generous. In Central Europe radiocarbon dates suggest a range of 1,500 years, say between 4200 and 2700 B.C. No comparable estimates can yet be made for the remaining provinces.

(i) THE STARČEVO CULTURE OF THE BALKANS

Farmers, characterized by the types thus designated, are recognizable in peninsular Greece both on the west coast (on Levkas) and in Thessaly and probably all along the north coasts of the Aegean to Gallipoli. Thence settlements extend right across the Balkan range in Macedonia and Bulgaria to the Danube. North of that river they can be traced up the Tisza to the Körös and into Transylvania to the head waters of the Maros and the Oltu, while east of the Carpathians they have been identified as far north as the head waters of the Seret and Prut and the Middle Dniestr.

Starčevo folk combined shifting cultivation with the breeding of kine, sheep, goats, and pigs, and with hunting and fishing. They are only known to have cultivated one-corn wheat and millet, both cereals indigenous to the Southern Balkans. Perhaps at first they planted grain between the forest trees after burning off the brushwood, changing their plots every year and shifting their settlements periodically – an extravagant system practised quite recently in Corsica and Liguria. In any case most Starčevo settlements consisted of clusters of small lean-to huts and seem to have been occupied only for a brief period. But south of the Balkan range the later Starčevo villages became more permanent and consisted of commodious and substantial houses, frequently rebuilt on the same place till village sites grew into tells (mounds). Perhaps these villagers had learned a system of rotation: to clear patches of forest with fire, to allow scrub to grow up again when the soil showed signs of exhaustion, and then to burn off the brushwood once more; the ash layer left by each burning acts as a fertilizer and permits the growth of a new crop on the same patch.[38] This system requires a lot of land, since plots must be left fallow for seven or more years and throughout that time must be protected from grazing stock. It is perhaps just as likely that the later Starčevo farmers had already learned a rotation between crop and pasture such as has to be assumed for Hither Asia in Halafian times and for the Balkans in Middle Neolithic.

Hunting and fishing were still vital to the subsistence economy of these farmers. Hunters did not use flint-tipped arrows, but presumably relied on the sling. For fishing along the rivers, nets were employed. We do not know whether they were individually or communally owned nor can we decide the same issue in respect of crops from the disposition of the small clay-lined silos in which they were stored.

The Starčevo farmers had inherited from unidentified Oriental ancestors querns and ovens for processing cereals, but for reaping them they gave a specifically Balkan form to the Near Eastern flint-toothed sickle and developed an original bone spatula for handling flour. For wood-working adzes were preferred, as in Hither Asia, to axes which were favoured in Egypt. But Starčevo pottery, highly sophisticated and sometimes adorned with painted designs,

45

resembles only remotely some Levantine neolithic. Mattocks of red deer antler alone might be claimed as a heritage from native mesolithic traditions. Though a spiral was occasionally painted on Starčevo vases, it was never used as a repetition pattern as it was by contemporary Danubians.

The villages, scattered about among the forests in this highly diversified Starčevo province, were yet not mutually isolated. Communications, conventionally classified as 'trade', are objectively documented by the distribution throughout the region of ornaments made from the shells of *Spondylus gaederopi*, a Mediterranean mussel, and by the transportation of Hungarian or Transylvanian obsidian to villages on the Prut and the Dniestr.

Social institutions, including warfare, are not positively illustrated by any available evidence, but some ritual equipment does survive. Female statuettes should have been used in fertility ceremonies and represent the same Mother Goddess as among Oriental peasantries. But in Starčevo villages neither she nor any other deity was worshipped in a durable temple nor served by a professional priesthood. On the contrary 'cult rooms' have been reported from ordinary farmhouses.[39] No ceremonial burials attest a cult of ancestral spirits in the underworld. But clay stamps may be regarded as ideological. They certainly look like copies of Asiatic stone seals and some bear the filled cross motive, very popular on seals in Hither Asia. Now these seals are accepted from Halafian times as evidence of private property in articles of commerce. But no sealings have been found in Starčevo or other European neolithic sites. So perhaps the European clay stamps, like similar ones from Jarmo (p. 36) and the Levantine Neolithic, were really used for multiplying magic motives on human bodies; European clay stamps have traditionally been called *pintadere* on the assumption that they were so used in painting the person.

Still the idea of their use and some motives that they bear were in all likelihood transmitted to Europe from Hither Asia.

(ii) THE MEDITERRANEAN CARDIAL CULTURE

An equally original adjustment to a purely Mediterranean environment is seen in a culture defined and labelled for archaeologists by its pottery. The latter was everywhere, but not exclusively, decorated with impressions made with the serrated edge of a *Cardium* shell and is therefore known as Cardial Ware. This pottery is found in Sicily and Malta, on the Tremiti and Aeolian Islands as well as all round the Mediterranean coasts in South Italy, along the Italian and French Riviera, and on the coasts of South France, Eastern Spain, and Little Africa. It is usually recovered from inhabited caves, a circumstance that unduly exaggerates the pastoral character of its makers; for parties of huntsmen and herdsmen often shelter in caves even when they live in regular villages. Actually Cardial folk, though they did hunt and fish and breed stock, also cultivated barley. Indeed they not only milled their grain on querns, but also ladled the flour with the same sort of bone spatulas as their kinsmen in the Balkans. In Liguria, South France, Spain, and Africa the huntsmen used bows and arrows armed with geometric microliths like those of mesolithic precursors in the same regions.

The distribution of sites on the North Coasts of the Mediterranean and on quite tiny islands leaves no doubt that the neolithic colonists had come by sea in boats. And after establishing themselves on shore they kept up maritime pursuits. Fishing expeditions developed into trading ventures. So obsidian from Lipari was transported as far as Liguria. Indeed the occupation of the volcanic Aeolian

Islands which, though very fertile, lack any permanent water supplies, must have been motivated by the desire for this admirable industrial material; the colonists must always have depended on bartering obsidian for necessities produced by kindred groups on the Italian mainland or Sicily.

Only in South-eastern Sicily and perhaps in Apulia do we know of domestic sites other than caves, and they were occupied not by the first colonists but by descendants – not certainly pure[40] – who had at least developed peculiar local styles of pottery – in Sicily Stentinello ware – in addition to the universal Cardial ware. The Sicilian villages were located close to the shore and girt by a rock-cut ditch and an internal palisade. The actual houses were probably round. Only in South France do some caves used as ossuaries for collective burial give a clue to Cardial ideology.

Save for the tiny islands, all the territories colonized by Cardial herdsmen were already populated by mesolithic savages. These could have contributed to the Cardial culture arrows armed with microliths and perhaps even sheep and goats. The cows and the barley must have been brought in the boats of the colonists and with them presumably the secret of making pots. Now a shell edge was regularly used for decorating the Levantine neolithic pottery, but shells or 'combs' giving a similar effect were widely used also in Africa as far south as Khartoum in the Sudan and Tibesti in the central Sahara. Moreover, round houses are generally regarded as African rather than Asiatic. On the other hand, Cardial ware may have been current in Greece before the Starčevo culture developed there[41] and in South Italy and Sicily vases, identical with unpainted Starčevo pots, are associated with the local Cardial ware.

On the scanty evidence at our disposal the neolithic constituents of the Cardial culture could equally well be derived from Northern Africa, from the coasts of Hither Asia, or from the Southern Balkan peninsula. In any case they came to be blended with mesolithic European elements, albeit to varying degrees, since recognizable mesolithic survivals, such as microliths, are by no means universally associated with Cardial ware. The latter symbolizes a unique culture adapted exclusively to the Mediterranean zone – it is nowhere found more than fifty miles from the coast – and profiting by the privileges of that sea for navigation.

(iii) THE DANUBIAN CULTURE CYCLE

The Danubian I culture is the best known in Neolithic Europe. It came to occupy a vast territory extending from the Bakony range in Hungary and the Vag-Nitra valleys in Slovakia northwards to the Maas in Holland, the edge of the Last Ice Age's moraines in Germany, and just to the Baltic coast east of the Oder and from the Belgian Meuse right to the Upper Vistula and thence round the northern flanks of the Carpathians to the Dniestr and the upper Prut. Danubian settlement was not, of course, continuous throughout this area; for it was rigidly confined to the löss-clad lowlands and valley slopes save between the Oder and the Vistula. Nor are all settlements strictly contemporary. The gradual colonization of such an enormous tract was the corollary both of the fertility of peasant families and of an extravagant and ill-balanced rural economy.

The Danubians were essentially farmers, but judging by their food refuse, largely vegetarian. They did indeed breed a few cows, pigs, goats, and sheep, but probably kept them tethered by day and stalled at night. The rich game resources of their habitat were curiously neglected; no recognizable hunting equipment and very few bones of game survive in their villages. But the Danubians cultivated one-corn, emmer, and a hexaploid wheat and barley together with beans, peas, lentils, and flax. They grew their crops on plots in the forest, cleared with fire and stone adzes, and tilled with hoes.[38] After two or three harvests such plots became exhausted and were abandoned. Another plot was then cleared and sown and in turn abandoned. When all land within convenient walking distance of the village had been used up by a repetition of this process, the whole settlement was removed to a fresh tract of virgin soil where the cycle could begin again. The original village was deserted till the clearings round it had all reverted to woodland; then the villagers might return to the old site and repeat the former cycle.

The farmers lived in villages comprising at most twenty long houses. The latter were substantial gabled halls with walls of split saplings and wattle-work, daubed with clay and supported by stout posts. The long houses varied from 18 to 22 feet in width and in length from 30 to 130 feet, with an average of 70 feet. Though these buildings doubtless served also as stables and granaries, the human household must have been something larger than a 'natural family' -- a lineage or a small clan. A village should then have comprised at least 200 souls; 600 might be nearer the mark. Either figure would mean a quite revolutionary growth of population in a region of interminable forest where only a few tiny bands of hunters had previously roamed. Contemporary houses in a Danubian village are all strictly parallel; to that extent the village was planned. But the planning was not done by a single potent chief; even Nazi excavators regretfully failed to find a precursor of der Führer in the oldest village on German soil. Danubian carpenters, like their Balkan contemporaries, employed stone adzes to the exclusion of axes. Their women-folk made simple pots which in form look just like copies of natural vessels cut out of gourds. Some, too, were decorated with linear patterns imitating the basketry cradles in which gourd vessels are carried. But other pots are freely decorated all over with spirals or maeanders used to make a repetition pattern as by the mammoth-hunters of Mezin (p. 24).

Though dispersed through primeval forests intercourse was maintained between the scattered villages. Many of these were located near streams that would be navigable for light craft; they served not only as routes through the dense oakwoods, but even as channels for trade. So stones for querns were brought from near Mayenne down the Moselle and Rhine and up the Meuse to the vicinity of Liège; even pots were transported from the mouth of the Main fifty miles down the Rhine to a Danubian village near Cologne. Though there is no direct evidence for industrial specialization within or between communities, some peasants may have increased their wealth or prestige by acting as traders; hoards of stone adze-blades have been picked up, mostly on the edge of the Danubian province, and they do look very like the hoards of metal ware that during the subsequent Bronze Age admittedly represent the stock in trade of travelling merchant-artificers. In any case some such trade did bring the Danubians materials, and doubtless ideas too, from outside their own huge province. Ornaments made from the same *Spondylus* shell from the Mediterranean that was so coveted among the Starčevo farmers of the Balkans reached Danubian villages even on the Middle Rhine and the Middle Oder.

The Danubian peasants seem to have been a peaceful folk; they have left no obviously military weapons. Even early villages were of course fenced against wild beasts; only the latest were defended against human aggressors. That is not to say that the whole Danubian province was a political unit; that, for all we can tell, was the village community. Within it there are no indications of differences of rank. By analogy with recent barbarians kinship within the family and society should have been matrilineal. But there is no positive evidence of matriarchy. Even female figurines, such as were so conspicuous among neolithic farmers in the Near East, were not made – or at least not of baked clay. Conventional representations of a human figure, not conspicuously sexed, adorn a few vases, but these are late and may be inspired by Danubian II influences.

Nor was funerary ritual highly elaborated. Ceremonial burials are rare, and only near the limits of Danubian expansion do they form regular cemeteries. On the Rhine these consist of inhumations in the contracted attitude, but on the Dniestr and on the Main cremation burials have been reported.

The Danubians' livestock and cereals must have been brought from further south, as neither lived wild north of the Balkans; the one-corn wheat points explicitly to Asia Minor or the Balkans. Their pronounced affection for *Spondylus* shells must have been inherited from ancestral societies living near the Mediterranean. Their pots simulate the gourd vessels presumably used by pre-pottery neolithic ancestors south-east of the Bakony, since north of that range gourds will not harden. But the maeander repetition patterns that adorn them surely revive artistic traditions handed down in basketry versions over the millennia from palaeolithic communities that had hunted mammoths on the same löss lands! But only in the latest Danubian settlements, belonging in time to period II, do flint microliths suggest a blending of native mesolithic traditions with those of the peasant colonists.

The Danubian Culture Cycle

Danubian society as we know it crystallized out somewhere on the Middle and Upper Danube and thence spread westward, northward, and eastward — on the Dniestr Danubians arrive only after Starčevo farmers. Their culture was a very successful adaptation to the Central European environment so long as there seemed to be unlimited land to colonize and cultivate.

(iv) WAS THERE ALSO A 'WESTERN NEOLITHIC' CYCLE?

A fourth stream of neolithic farmers, coming immediately from North Africa, may, according to some authorities, have been responsible for the Almeria culture that existed in Spain side by side with the Cardial, and for the little-known Dolmen culture of Portugal. An extension of this current north of the Pyrenees would then have formed the core of a vague Western culture-cycle concretely represented by the Chassean of South and Central France, the Cortaillod culture of Switzerland, and the Windmill Hill culture of the British Isles. The latter manifestations are not tangible till Middle Neolithic, and everywhere the exotic neolithic elements are hard to disentangle from autochthonous mesolithic survivals. For the whole of Western Europe was relatively well populated with mesolithic hunter-fishers, some of whom (e.g. the Tardenoisians) may themselves have been immigrants from Africa. Some of them, though they made no pots, may have been breeding small horned cattle and oxen. Postponing to the next chapter the Western culture north of the Pyrenees, we must consider here only what it might have derived from Africa through its supposed Peninsular ancestor.

The case may be very superficially summarized as follows: Almost identical assemblages of microlithic flints and leathery pots are found in North African habitation sites [42] and in farmers' villages in Almeria. The Almerians lived in round or oval huts and may have cultivated olives in addition to cereals. They buried their dead in cave ossuaries but also, individually or collectively, in chambers of stone slabs covered with round cairns. The Portuguese 'dolmens' (never properly described up to date) seem to have been similar chambers under cairns that contained a single corpse accompanied again by leathery pots and geometric microliths. In North Africa pastoral tribes – admittedly at an uncertain date – also piled cairns over stone chambers (likewise always known as 'dolmens')[43] in which perhaps only chiefs were buried. Finally the lively paintings of Eastern Spain, some of which depict tame sheep, stylistically look very African, as remarked on p. 24.

So bands of herdsmen, driven to cross the Straits of Gibraltar by the desiccation of the Sahara, may have introduced domestic stock, cereals, and neolithic traditions which they themselves had acquired in the Nile valley. The North African and Almerian pots are in fact quite like early Egyptian ones; the stone tombs under round cairns in all three areas might be barbarized versions of the mudbrick monuments erected over the tombs of the earliest pharaohs in Upper Egypt.[44] One of the North African settlements in question has been radio-carbon dated about 3050 B.C., a figure agreeing well with the historical dates for the first pharaohs. The foregoing account is admittedly highly speculative and must in any case be grossly oversimplified. Yet something along those lines seems needed to explain traditions of domestic and funerary architecture peculiar to Western Europe.

During phase i four great provinces of Europe had been colonized by neolithic farmers. These created as many cultures – or culture-cycles – as first adjustments to European environments. Since in all four novel exotic elements predominated over recognizable survivals of the native mesolithic heritage, they may be termed Primary Neolithic cultures. In Phase II the area of primary colonization was further extended. But the uniform Primary cultures break up into an embarrassing number of small regional cultures by divergent adaptation to local conditions. At the same time the penetration of fresh Oriental ideas and even the intrusion of further immigrant groups from the Near East accelerated diversification. Finally the adoption by aboriginal food-gatherers of the neolithic economy and appropriate items of equipment from the Primary cultures, resulted in the emergence of Secondary Neolithic cultures;[45] in all these, traits inherited from the previous food-gathering stage are recognizable, if not predominant.

CHAPTER 5

ADAPTATIONS TO EUROPEAN ENVIRONMENTS

(i) THE BALKANS AND SOUTH ITALY

QUICKENING impulses from the cradle of food-production are naturally most conspicuous in the Balkan peninsula. But, it must be recalled, Middle Neolithic in Temperate Europe may not have begun before the Urban Revolution in Egypt and Mesopotamia. So some of the Oriental contributions detected at this stage may be just reflections of the penetration of Europe by the international trade that the Revolution had engendered. No such suspicion affects the Sesklo culture [37] of Peninsular Greece and Western Macedonia which demonstrably emerged before the first detectable contacts with the new Oriental civilizations. With its fine kiln-fired pots, gaily decorated with basketry patterns in shiny paint, its clay sling bullets, its stone bowls, its ritual paraphernalia of terracotta figurines, and models of animals, houses, and furniture, and its stamps of baked clay or even stone, the Sesklo culture looks like the result of a bodily transfer of Hassuna-Halafian traditions from Hither Asia across the Aegean that might well have been effected by a fresh immigration of Asiatic peasants. But nothing like the Halafian temples has been identified in Greece and *Spondylus* shell continued popular for ornaments. The rural economy probably now included the cultivation of fruit trees as well as cereals and very likely transhumance of livestock to mountain pastures during the summers. It certainly provided for some rotation that permitted the continuous occupation of permanent villages of mud-brick houses. In Otzaki Mound [41], one of the tells formed from the repeated rebuildings of such a village, Sesklo types occur in occupation levels above those yielding Cardial and Starčevo pottery. But below, and therefore before, these latter are ruins of a settlement characterized by painted pottery that might be ancestral to Sesklo ware.

In the central Balkans Asiatic traditions in ritual equipment, the manufacture of stone bowls and clay stamps, and the use of ovens are just as prominent in the Vinča culture.[37] It is represented in tells – the sites of permanent villages continuously inhabited through two periods (Vinča I and Vinča II) – from Western Macedonia up the Vardar and down the Morava to the Serbian Danube and beyond that river across the Banat and up the Maros to Tordos in Transylvania. But Vinča pottery was not painted, but self-coloured and decorated, albeit only in Vinča II, with spiral and maeander repetition patterns. This later Vinča decorarive art reputedly results from the adoption by the farmers of aesthetic traditions derived, directly or through 'Danubian' neighbours, from the palaeolithic mammoth-hunters of the löss lands. Antler harpoons and mattocks, used by Vinča folk for fishing and chopping, might also have been inherited from unidentified mesolithic natives. Yet good analogues to Vinča I pottery are available on both sides of the Aegean and in the Levant. Now in the last-named area they, like analogues to Cardial ware (p. 48), belong to the earlier neolithic, prior to the introduction of pottery painted in Hassuna-Halafian styles. West of the Aegean, on the contrary, in the Larisa culture the self-coloured wares replace and succeed those painted in Sesklo style and akin to the Halafian. So from pottery seemingly contradictory inferences have been drawn – either an immigration from Hither Asia into Greece and thence up the Vardar or an nvasion of Peninsular Greece from the Middle Danube basin down that river! Here a decision is neither possible nor necessary.

Still, an incursion from north of the Balkans does seem the most likely explanation of the Dimini culture of Eastern Thessaly and Corinthia. Here the intruders expelled or subjugated the Sesklo villagers, betraying their North Balkan origin by the spirals and maeanders painted on their technically inferior pots, by their employment of antler mattocks or axes, and perhaps by their domestic architecture, though preserving the same sort of ideological equipment. If the newcomers really built the fortifications round their hill-top villages and the little palaces enclosed therein, they could be regarded as a conquering aristocracy ruling subject Sesklo populations but themselves ruled by embryo kings. But the palaces and fortification walls may have been built much later by a new wave of invaders who arrived about 1800 B.C.

On the Lower Danube equally sedentary peasant societies, who cultivated emmer as well as one-corn wheat, created the Boian culture, which replaces Starčevo on both sides of the river. In the preference for adzes and slings and affection for ornaments of *Spondylus* shell they maintained older local traditions. But no clay figurines or other models illustrate the Asiatic fertility cult, and pots were unpainted. They were, however, decorated with maeander repetition patterns as elsewhere on the South-east European löss lands.

Asiatic elements are not recognizable at all in the cultures of South Italy and Sicily and the Aeolian Islands that came to replace the Cardial and Stentinello. The painted pottery that distinguishes them is generally supposed to have been introduced by colonists from the Balkans, but these did not bring female figurines or the associated ritual equipment. On the other hand round huts should be African in origin, and though round huts were inhabited in neolithic Cyprus, the rural economy foreshadows what is familiar during the Iron Age in the British Isles and elsewhere in the Celtic West. For the round huts, each in its own fenced yard, were grouped in villages encircled by defensive ditches, or stood alone. But both villages and lone steadings stood within much larger enclosures, similarly defended. A lone steading plainly represents the farmhouse with its yard and cultivated 'in-field' held by an individual proprietor, while the enclosed area round each village must have been the open communal field in which each villager held a plot for one season, only the farmyards being owned by individual households. Archaeology gives no hint as to the political relations between the peasant villagers and the individual farmers or between the several villages themselves.

(ii) THE DANUBIAN PROVINCE AND ITS EXTENSIONS

North of the Maros and the Drave and throughout the old Danubian province, a persistence of shifting cultivation prevented the establishment of villages permanent enough for their ruins to form tells. Yet a better balanced rural economy may be deduced from the multiplication of flocks and herds, now presumably allowed to graze freely in the clearings, while the regions' natural resources were more fully exploited by hunting and fishing. Since farming was still restricted to the löss areas, the natural growth of populations and the recruitment of fresh farmers from Secondary Neolithic communities resulted in an incipient pressure on the land. The shortage of cultivable plots would be further accentuated by free-grazing stock; for they would prevent the regeneration of the forest so that former clearings could no longer be refertilized by simply burning down the scrub that would otherwise have covered them. Finally livestock represent a prize for raiders. As a result of these factors the institution of war is not unexpectedly recognizable in phase II both in the Danubian province and elsewhere. Many Danubian II villages were defended by stout palisades and deep ditches to keep off attackers. Still there are yet no evidences for war chiefs in the Danubian province unless perforated stone hammer-axes be emblems of authority.

Everywhere indeed the communal long houses of Danubian I were replaced by smaller two-roomed dwellings, measuring overall 21 to 30 feet by 15 to 16 feet, and provided with ovens in each room. These are, of course, better suited to a natural pairing family. But it cannot be proved that this was yet patriarchal. On the contrary the Danubian II cultures in Central Europe had adopted, as wholeheartedly as Sesklo and Vinča, the Oriental fertility rituals that used figurines of the Mother Goddess and models of animals, birds, houses and furniture.

Danubian II cultures in the proper sense extend from the Save and the Upper Tisza across Hungary, Slovakia, Lower Austria and Moravia to the Upper Vistula in Poland and the Upper Elbe in Bohemia. They are characterized archaeologically by a liking for coloured vases, but, in contrast to Greece and South Italy, the colours usually were not fast, painted on the light surface of the vase before firing, but white, red, or yellow daubed on a black ground after firing. The patterns include spirals and maeanders, but also basketry designs. Clay stamps now came into use even in Moravia and Bohemia. The old international trade still brought to the area a supply of *Spondylus* shell from the Mediterranean, but perhaps also manufactures from the urbanized industries of the Near East and Crete. Together with local obsidian, copper trinkets, made from equally local copper, were also distributed. Ores and even native copper were certainly available in Hungary and might have been discovered by Danubian farmers. But prospectors from the Orient may already have been exploring the region and revealed their value to its barbarian inhabitants.

Beyond the limits indicated in the last paragraph Danubian I culture persisted unchanged save for the fortification of the villages. But it was juxtaposed to, and interdigitated with, Secondary Neolithic Danubian cultures, labelled 'Stroke-ornamented', 'Rössen', 'Hinkelstein', etc. In all these Danubian traditions in economy and industrial equipment were blended with others represented by geometric microliths, extended or cremation burials, that may be attributed to various autochthonous groups of hunter-fishers, acculturated by the Primary Danubian immigrants. All were more warlike and engaged more in hunting than the Danubian I peasants, while the domestic architecture and social organization of the Rössen folk at least was Danubian II rather than Danubian I.

At the same time the province was extended westward: Danubian I peasants spread from Belgium to the Marne and even the Paris basin; Rössen farmers from the Main advanced up the Rhine into the Alpine foothills to Liechtenstein above the Lake of Constance. South-westward farmers, crossing the Julian Alps in search of land, carried rather mixed Danubian II traditions into Upper Italy and thence to the Mediterranean coasts. In Ligurian caves Mother Goddess figurines, clay stamps, vases decorated with spirals, and ornaments of *Spondylus* shell proclaim the dominance of Danubian II traditions in a local culture that succeeded the Cardial.

East of the Carpathians an extension of Danubian culture formed the principal constituent in a distinctive adaptation to the severely continental conditions of these parklands. The resultant, named Tripolye, after a site near Kiev, succeeded Starčevo, Boian, and Danubian I settlements on the ⟍

61

Upper Oltu, the Prut, and the Dniestr, and carried over traditions from these and from unidentified hunter-fishers and perhaps steppe pastoralists too. It endured for a long time and developed through three distinguishable phases during which it spread to the Dniepr and the edge of the grassy steppes. The economy was still based on shifting cultivation, so no villages were occupied long enough to form tells, though some sites were reoccupied after intervals during which scrub could grow up again. Crops, stored in great jars in each house, were owned severally by individual households, though the land may have been held in common. Stock-breeding, hunting, fishing, and collecting made equal contributions to the food supply. In the first phase most of the meat eaten was game, but the proportion of domestic animals' bones in the food refuse steadily increases during subsequent periods. Moreover horses, at first perhaps only hunted, had probably been tamed by the last phase; they certainly provided meat, perhaps then also milk and motive power.[46] Sledges for them to draw are attested by models, but not wheeled vehicles.

Tripolye farmers lived in substantial houses with floors and walls of split timbers, heavily plastered with clay. They comprised two to five rooms and were furnished with large ovens and also cruciform pediments or altars. Russian prehistorians regard the larger houses as enlargements of a two-roomed unit to accommodate married children. Each would then represent a joint household or great family of a type that survived among the Southern Slavs into this century.[47] A normal village would consist of thirty to forty-five houses arranged radially on the circumference of an irregular circle 600 to 1,600 feet in diameter, defended by steep ravines supplemented by ditch and rampart.

Trade brought to the Moldavian and Ukrainian villagers across the Carpathians obsidian from Hungary or Transylvania and also copper and a little gold. Bangles and smaller trinkets of unalloyed copper were being worn already in the earliest phase; later became available flat axes, pickaxes, and daggers, such as on the Middle Danube are Late Neolithic III. Though Tripolye potters' kilns would produce a temperature sufficient to melt copper, no traces of metal-working have been observed in Tripolye villages. Perhaps the villagers secured their metal ware from prospectors who would have shipped the bulk of their winnings to Oriental markets from undiscovered Black Sea ports. Domestic potters built by hand and fired in kilns magnificent pots gaily decorated with painted patterns – at first spirals and maeanders in the familiar löss-land style which later disintegrate.

Tripolye societies shared with Danubian II and earlier Balkan communities the whole ideology expressed in female figurines and models of animals, houses, chairs, and couches as well as clay stamps. The positions of figurines within the houses and the cruciform pediments or altars in this case positively attest the domestic character of this cult. On the other hand, clay phalli and the prominence of the bull in plastic art show that the rôle of the male in procreation was appreciated and ritually applied. That should at least foreshadow the transition to a patriarchal order for which there is, however, no positive evidence.

(iii) WESTERN AND NORTHERN EUROPE

By Neolithic II at least 'Western cultures', or at least distinctive leathery pots that should characterize them, become tangible to illustrate adjustments to the varied environments of Atlantic Europe north of the Pyrenees.

Their neolithic elements might be derived from a northward thrust of Almerians, if not borrowed from Cardial
herdsmen or infiltrating Danubian and Rössen peasants.
Everywhere mesolithic survivals are conspicuous; hunting
and stock-breeding are more prominent than in the
Danubian rural economy; flint mines and axe-factories
may – but need not – indicate some intercommunal
specialization. In general axes were preferred to adzes,
while female figurines were only very exceptionally
modelled in clay. Still there is no single Western culture,
but a cycle of local cultures of which only two need be
particularized.

Cortaillod farmers inhabited rectangular two-roomed
houses of Danubian II plan strung out along the shores of
Alpine lakes – the old belief that they were built on piles
above the waters has now been rejected by most Swiss
specialists – or on the treeless, peat-covered beds of dried-up
meres. They cultivated the usual cereals – including one-
corn wheat – probably still without a plough, and kept
cows, goats, and sheep that were tethered and in winter
stalled. Neither ceremonial burials nor other manifestations
of ritual behaviour have been recorded, nor are differences
of rank within the villages observable. A reliable radio-
carbon estimate dates a very early Cortaillod settlement in
Switzerland about 2750 B.C., though farmers had been
cultivating Swiss soil from unidentified dry-land settlements
a good deal earlier. But Cortaillod farmers were still living,
in the Jura at least, as late as 2400 B.C.

The Windmill Hill culture, according to Piggott,[48] is
first manifested on the chalk downs of southern England
whence it spread, gradually and probably reinforced by
fresh impulses from the Continent, all over the British
Isles. A radio-carbon estimate puts its arrival as far away
as Cumberland as early as 2900 B.C., but English prehis-

torians almost unanimously reject this date as far too high. These pioneers of British farming grew wheat – including a little one-corn – in preference to the hardier barley, but relied still more on breeding cattle and pigs together with a few goats and sheep; game they curiously neglected. Clusters of one or two rectangular houses are known, but no regular villages. 'Causewayed camps' – hill-tops girt with two or more interrupted ditches – in Southern England are regarded by Piggott as cattle-kraals rather than fortified settlements. Flint was won in Southern England by miners skilled at sinking shafts through solid chalk and cutting underground galleries. Axes were manufactured at outcrops of suitable rock in Cumberland, Antrim, and North-West Wales, and exported even to Southern England and Scotland. But this remarkable trade and perhaps even flint-mining, according to Piggott, did not begin effectively before the advent of the Beaker-folk that in this book marks the beginning of Late Neolithic III.

The ideology and something of the sociology of the Windmill Hill population is – very imperfectly – disclosed by a few human figurines and models of phalli, very roughly carved out of lumps of chalk, and by ceremonial burials. The best known are simultaneous collective burials under long barrows – mounds sometimes as much as 300 feet long and often broader and higher at one end than the other. At the wider end the unburnt or cremated bones of one or more corpses are heaped together on a low platform of chalk or within a kerb of flint nodules. In the stupendous funerary monuments the number of interments seems disproportionately small; four long barrows held only one each, twenty-five is the maximum. Long barrows can hardly be the tombs of individual peasants nor yet communal ossuaries for a whole village; they look more like the sepulchres of chiefs and their families. In that case small

cemeteries of cremation burials in circular enclosures, girt
by a ditch and an external bank, might contain the graves
of commoners. Admittedly these circular enclosures,
termed class I henges, contain British Secondary Neolithic
as well as Windmill Hill relics. Yet, together with cursūs –
narrow enclosures from one to six miles in length – they
represent a peculiarly British elaboration of an ideology
the embryo of which might be Western. Long barrows on
the other hand are more likely to be Northern or ultimately
Danubian.[49]

Finally, the colonization by farmers of the great plain of
Northern Europe only began at a time when the Danubian
province, the Balkans, and the Mediterranean coasts had
already been occupied and adaptive specialization had
begun; the radio-carbon age of the earliest dated settlement
in Denmark is only 2650 B.C. The northern environment of
heavily wooded boulder clays, glacial sands and marine
deposits, and a cold damp climate presented an exceptionally
severe challenge to neolithic farmers. A highly successful
adaptation to it was achieved, after two or three periods of
development (Northern I and II or TRB A, B, and C), in the
First Northern or TRB (*Tragtbaeger*, funnel-beaker) culture.
It is best known in Denmark and South Sweden, the regions
most propitious – or least unpropitious – for neolithic farming, but seemingly also the most densely populated by
mesolithic hunter-fishers of Maglemose and Ertebølle
ancestry. Arriving among the latter in Denmark in phase
A the colonizing pioneers, practising shifting cultivation,
perversely planted one-corn, emmer and hexaploid wheats
in preference to barley and kept their stock tethered, feeding
them on leaves through the long winters. An ideology,
distinctive of the whole First Northern cycle, found expression in offerings cast into bogs – human victims, animals,
pots, flint implements, and amber beads.

In phase B these pioneers were followed by more pastoral colonists. These cleared larger tracts of woodland with fire to produce pastures for free-grazing stock as much as plots for cultivation. Yet these herdsmen did not linger long enough in one place to prevent the ultimate regeneration of the forest, but in a few generations burned their way across Denmark and South Sweden till they had nearly reached Stockholm on the Baltic coast. On the Continent neither phases A and B nor cultivating and herding groups can be distinguished as yet, but farmers of either group can be recognized by a few distinctive pots and flint implements, and bog-offerings between the Vistula and the Elbe. These might mark the track of an immigration from Byelorussia or still further east. It is more economical to regard the First Northern as a Secondary Neolithic culture resulting from the acculturation of local food-gatherers by the immigrant Danubian peasants who had in fact advanced across the Plain to the Baltic between the Vistula and Oder. The composition of the First Northerners' crops is actually Danubian and their chieftains' tombs look like ceremonial copies of Danubian long houses. But neither their ideology nor any item in their material equipment is the least Danubian; for instance they used flint axes instead of greenstone adzes and arrows armed with transverse microlithic heads and buried their dead extended on their backs. Such behaviour carries on local mesolithic traditions as exemplified in the Danish Ertebølle culture.

Before the end of Neolithic II, i.e. in TRB C or Northern II, the whole North European plain from the Vistula to the Rhine was dominated by warlike groups of First Northern farmers, differentiated one from another by divergent adjustments to local conditions expressed in peculiarities of ceramic decoration and burial rites. Kindred groups appear to have spread southwards as far as the Danube in Lower

Austria and westward at least to Switzerland and Belgium; even the British Windmill Hill culture may be attributed to one of these as well as to colonists from South France.[49] But in Central Europe these First Northern bands encountered and mingled with Danubian communities, sacrificing most of their own traditions. On the plain itself the distinctive lineaments of the First Northern culture in TRB C stand out most clearly in Denmark.

There the culture of phase C owes more to the cultivators of phase A than to the herdsmen of B. The farmers lived in one-roomed huts aligned in rows to form villages. At Barkaer fifty-eight such huts were set close side by side in two rows with an open space between them, for all the world like nineteenth-century colliers' rows. The commonest burial practice was individual interment in the extended attitude in a simple earth grave; five such graves had been dug under house floors at Barkaer. But in Poland and North Germany as well as Denmark some persons were thus buried in narrow chambers formed of planks, of stone slabs on edge, or of huge erratic boulders. The chamber was covered by a mound, in Denmark round or long and rectangular, in Germany and Poland trapezoid in plan like a British long barrow. And, like the latter, the length of the mound is everywhere out of all proportion to the size of the burial chamber at one end. All three types of barrow probably simulate houses of the living. The Northern long barrows would then imitate Danubian I long houses – some of these were rectangular in plan, others trapezoid, just like the barrows. Such monumental tombs must have been built for chieftains, though commoners' graves are regrettably rare. The chiefs presumably owed their authority to warlike prowess rather than sanctity, and may even have taken a step towards kingship by subjugating other communities of farmers or aborigina food-gatherers. Funnily enough these putative war-chiefs disappear from the archaeological record in Northern III – TRB D when 'missionaries' from the West had introduced some version of the Megalithic Religion (p. 125). Then closed burial chambers were replaced by equally monumental tombs, provided with an entrance passage and used as genuinely communal ossuaries.

Even in Northern II TRB societies were imbued with martial traditions. In addition to bows and arrows, warriors brandished battle-axes of stags' antler, copper imitations of these, or stone versions of the metal axes. They might just as well be called commercially minded. First Northern communities controlled the Jutland deposits of amber – a fossil resin that becomes electrified by friction and which had been prized for this magic virtue even by mesolithic savages. Precious beads were traded at least as far as the Upper Oder and Vistula. In return for amber a few articles of copper reached Jutland even in Neolithic II from the Danubian province. In Poland Galician banded flint was mined and exported as far as Denmark, though perhaps not before Neolithic III. By that time at least another village [50] in Poland can be described as a community of expert axe-makers, manufacturing for the market.

Most First Northern farmers are generally regarded as hoe-cultivators. But among the Polish branch an ox-drawn plough was probably coming into use. There too have been found clay discs that look like the wheels of a model wagon. Finally bones of horses occur in several First Northern settlements; what look like the cheek-pieces of bridle bits,[50] if correctly interpreted, indicate that, once more in Poland, horses had been tamed for driving if not for riding. Ploughs, wheeled vehicles, and domesticated horses were innovations, pregnant with revolutionary possibilities. But the relative and absolute age of the above-mentioned hints of their appearance is highly problematical. They most probably are Late Neolithic and are not the least likely to be older than the ox-carts and horses of the Baden culture of Hungary. In the Orient wheeled vehicles and ploughs are indubitably substantially older.

We have indeed transgressed the limits of our Middle Neolithic and reached a point in sidereal time not only several centuries after the Urban Revolution had been completed in Egypt and Mesopotamia, but also after repercussions of that event had begun to react even on Temperate Europe. The copper trinkets from Danubian II, Tripolye, and First Northern sites are no older than sophisticated castings made by Sumerian smiths in temple cities , and monumental barrows in England and Poland are no older than the stately tombs of the first pharaohs. Indeed the rural economy attributed to the First Northern culture approximates to that of Period III in Central Europe more than to the Danubian II. Yet it is convenient to depart still further from the chronological order and mention two Central European cultures. Both maintained essentially Danubian traditions of farming, but a shift of emphasis in the direction of stock-breeding has intensified warlike behaviour and promoted changes in social structure and ideology.

The Bodrogkeresztur culture in Eastern Hungary and Transylvania might result from the further development of the Danubian II cultures of the same region. Substantial villages may be deduced from cemeteries of as many as 200 graves. These villagers were the first known local consumers of the products of a metallurgical industry that had been established in Transylvania and was now producing flat axes, daggers, and axe-adzes of native copper; the latter are miners' tools that could also be used as weapons. The distribution of metal ware was, however, so irregular that

Bodrogkeresztur farmers, like their Tripolye contemporaries, still had to rely so much on stone tools as to appear neolithic.

The Baden culture, occupying the western portion of the old Danubian province from the Save northwards to the Upper Vistula, the Upper Oder, and the Upper Elbe, might be styled Danubian III. The cultivation of cereals, still including one-corn and probably aided by a plough, was balanced with a dairy economy and the breeding of substantial flocks of sheep for wool as well as for mutton. Horses' bones are prominent in domestic refuse too. Four-wheeled wagons were available for transport, but probably drawn by oxen. While Baden equipment still looks neolithic, metal ornaments of explicitly Anatolian type constitute the first unambiguous links with an Asiatic school of metallurgy.

Baden farmers lived in large villages of one-roomed houses; each was occupied by a single patriarchal family, but the several families were distributed among two or more clans. Clan chiefs or village headmen enjoyed such prestige and sanctity that after death their bodies were conveyed to the grave on hearses that together with the draft oxen were buried with them – a ritual identical with that observed at the obsequies of the oldest Mesopotamian monarchs. Yet the Baden chiefs' graves lie within the village cemeteries and do not differ in kind from those of the remaining villagers. So their occupants were not so elevated above their fellow clansmen as to appear masters or kings rather than just leaders. In domestic fertility ceremonies the use of female figurines had fallen into abeyance, but models of bulls and rams, as of wagons, illustrate the survival of Danubian II traditions. At the same time a conception of ancestral spirits as helpers in fertilizing crops and herds may be implicit in a more elaborate funerary cere monial. The dead were sometimes cremated and the ashes inurned, more often inhumed, generally in cemeteries of single graves (over 300 graves have been recorded in a single cemetery), occasionally in collective family tombs.

The Baden culture might just express the adjustment of Danubian traditions to a more pastoral economy. Its metal ware may reflect merely the activities of Asiatic prospectors working within the orbit of Baden culture but outside its social organization. But a penetration of its very core can be deduced from wheeled vehicles associated with chieftains' burials. Yet if the Oriental invention and its ceremonial application were introduced by pastoral conquerors from the Pontic steppes, these were apparently not superimposed as a distinct ruling class upon the Danubian population, but accepted and absorbed thereby.

To conclude this excursus we must remind the reader of the persistence till this date and later of the savage economy of food-gathering throughout the great zone of tundra and coniferous forest extending from the Norwegian coasts right across Northern Eurasia. This vast tract of plains, where the severity of Arctic winters is tempered by no mountain screen from the Polar blasts, was uncongenial to neolithic farming. But it was well stocked with game – bears, elks, fur-bearing rodents – fowls and fish, while its Baltic and Oceanic coasts offered sea-mammals too. This wild food had supported an ingenious mesolithic population since 6000 B.C., and Maglemoseans had devised an efficient equipment for its exploitation. Hunter-fishers continued to employ it profitably till 2000 or 1000 B.C. – indeed in places till the present day. Of course since 6000 behaviour patterns had been modified and diversified and equipment had been improved. Specialization was needed to take the fullest advantage of local resources. So some coastal communities concentrated on the pursuit of sea mammals. Others in Norway began cod fishing;[51] fish were dried and very probably exported, as they are today. Trade in useful or magical substances – Scandinavian flint, Olonetz slate, porphyry from the Urals, amber from Sammland – was as extensive and as regular among the boreal hunter-fishers as among neolithic farmers in Temperate Europe; regular expeditions were organized to secure flint in Denmark and South Sweden and distributed axes made therefrom far into Norway, Northern Sweden, and Finland.

For land transport the Maglemoseans' light sleighs, drawn by men, had grown into heavier sledges drawn by dogs which were in use from Finland to the Urals by 2000 B.C. About 1000, reindeer sledges[52] had reached the Baltic; the domestication of the draft animals must have been effected earlier and in Siberia.[53] On water the skin boats, inferred for the Maglemoseans, are now illustrated in pictures on Scandinavian rocks. For hunting Maglemosean equipment was retained, but perfected; the Maglemosean reinforced bow was eventually replaced by the Turko-Mongolian composite bow strengthened with antler strips, which fired heavier arrows. For carpentry a splendid kit of stone gouges and adzes had been contrived. Almost everywhere the hunter-fishers had learned to make pots. Everywhere these were built up in rings by hand, ovoid in form, and decorated with pits. Additional patterns, made with whipped cords, a notched pebble stamp or a short-toothed bone comb, characterize the variety known as Pit-comb ware from the Baltic to the Urals; variations in the patterns help to define chronological phases and distinct tribal groups.

The dead were buried extended, often sprinkled with red ochre. Exceptional cemeteries of fifty graves on Gotland and 150 on Deer Island in Lake Onega disclose the size of communities that could live together on a basis of hunting and fishing, or at least that did resort to the same site for funerary ceremonies. In the Deer Island cemetery a few exceptional graves unambiguously belong to chiefs, while double or triple burials might imply a patriarchal family organization. Ideology found expression also in more or less naturalistic pictures painted or engraved on ice-smoothed rocks and in very lifelike carvings of animals and birds in wood, greenstone, flint, and bone. Game animals, birds, and fish were the favourite themes. But human figures too, of both sexes, were represented in the rock-drawings and modelled in clay, but always in a schematic manner.

The population of the European taiga was doubtless largely descended from the Maglemoseans of the Boreal phase. But they were certainly mixed with fresh immigrants, some at least from the Asiatic side of the Urals. Anthropologists have recognized persons of Mongoloid type as far west as Lake Onega. These may have introduced the new composite bow. Some may have spread further south and west to mingle with the peasantries of Central Europe amongst whom Mongoloid physical types have also been detected by the Bronze Age.

So before 2000 B.C. immigrant and native farmers had painfully penetrated the virgin forests and taken possession of the most suitable soils in Europe for cultivation and grazing. Three or four immigrant streams had introduced cereals and domestic stock. Mixed to an unknown degree with autochthonous food-gatherers, they had succeeded in adapting to Mediterranean and Temperate environments exotic plants and animals and had elaborated workable systems for their cultivation and multiplication. Early Neolithic rural economies, based on clearing a plot with fire only to abandon it after a couple of harvests, were of

course frightfully extravagant. None allowed the establishment of permanent villages, to be inhabited continuously
through several generations. The numbers who could live
together as a single village community were rigidly
restricted by the same factors to twenty or less large
households. With their rudimentary equipment and waste-
ful rural economy such tiny communities simply could not
regularly produce enough to guarantee a livelihood to a
single full-time specialist – not even a professional priest or
a professional chief.

No doubt all had elaborated ideologies, systems of beliefs
that gave them confidence to sustain unremitting toil and
fortitude in face of privations and disasters. No doubt too
experts were forthcoming to guide their productive
labours and their ritual behaviour. But cult remained
primarily a domestic affair, not celebrated in any permanent temple, and its ministers were hardly professionals.
The social surplus producible by any village was just
insufficient to relieve a priest or a headman or chief from
contributing physically to the communal food supply. The
very instability of the village was incompatible with the
erection of monumental temples.

The Middle Neolithic phase undoubtedly witnessed the
realization of better adjustments to the environment. But
even the improvements then effected did not allow any
substantial enlargement of the unit of settlement or, save
in Greece and the Balkans, the establishment of really
durable villages. None of these little groups could individually collect enough food to guarantee the subsistence of a
village priest, a village headman, or a village potter. All
able-bodied villagers must contribute actively and mate-
rially to the food supply if the group were to survive and
multiply. Now the villagers were distributed among quite
a large number of distinct societies which we have not had

75

space even to name. Their exclusive traditions in ritual behaviour and material culture must express complete political independence and linguistic separation, if not mutual hostility as well. The interposition of cultural frontiers in addition to physical obstacles did not indeed inhibit occasional intercourse – what we have termed 'trade'. Yet it probably reinforced the neolithic tradition of economic self-sufficiency. That is to say, a village community might be glad enough to obtain luxury articles, such as shells, from strangers by barter, but still shrink from becoming dependent on such traffic for raw materials essential for the manufacture of tools and weapons, to say nothing of food.

The multiplication of distinguishable cultures, of archaeologically recognizable societies, was not due just to the fission of the four great Early Neolithic cycles. It reflects an absolute expansion of the population as a result of the fecundity of the Primary immigrant farmers, of the conversion of food-gatherers to food-production by imitation of, or by incorporation in, farming societies, and of some fresh immigration. This expansion itself is of course testimony to the farmers' success in adapting themselves to European conditions. But that very success had brought them up against the contradiction that is inherent in any neolithic economy; there was no way of providing for their steadily multiplying families other than appropriating fresh land. Now quantitatively no doubt there was plenty of land for a population that was still absolutely minute. But of land that could be cleared by self-sufficing peasants with stone tools the limit was already in sight. Left to themselves, European communities could, and doubtless would, have continued in the old way of life, dodging their population problem by incessant wars in which the surplus young men killed each other off, as the Red Indians actually did in the similar environment of North America. But close to Europe in the Near East the unique solution had been found long before 2000 B.C., albeit at frightful cost. The results ultimately offered Europeans too a way of escape from their dilemma at a less grievous price.

CHAPTER 6

THE URBAN REVOLUTION
IN THE ORIENT

THE first step towards escape from the rigid limits of neolithic barbarism was the establishment of a metallurgical industry – an organization for the regular extraction, distribution, and processing of copper – and ideally of tin too to make bronze. That not only provided farmers with superior tools and weapons, but also offered their children new prospects of a livelihood and broke down the self-sufficiency of the neolithic village. But its establishment was a formidable task that could not be accomplished anywhere in Europe, but only in the Ancient East. There it overturned the barbarian social order, based on kinship, and evoked a new population of full-time specialists. The latter is my excuse for calling it the Urban Revolution.

Under a neolithic economy every adult member of every community was primarily engaged in producing the food requisite to feed himself and his children. The regular use of copper or bronze on the contrary presupposed the existence of a small army of full-time specialists, liberated from preoccupation with farming, fishing, or hunting to devote their whole time to mining and smelting ores, to transporting the winnings through deserts and forests, and to converting the metal by casting and forging into tools, weapons, vessels, or ornaments. The operations of mining, smelting, and casting are far more delicate, intricate, and exacting than any of the normal domestic tasks performed by neolithic peasants – even than mining flint nodules and flaking them or quarrying handy-sized blocks of rock for conversion into axes or querns. They were absorbing full-

78

time occupations. The operators could only work provided they were supported by the foodstuffs produced by the farmers or fishers from amongst whom they came. Indeed they must be assured of a generous reward if they were to be persuaded to abandon reliance on their own efforts to secure the essentials of life. The distributors might demand even stronger inducements. They had to transport the metal many days' journey across mountains and torrents, exposed to appalling hazards from wild beasts, alien societies, and malignant spirits. Unless the country he travelled through were uninhabited, the merchant would have to conciliate its human occupants and its guardian spirits with very substantial douceurs. He could justly demand a great deal more than the equivalent of the food consumed on the journey. In other words to get a metallurgical industry going a very substantial reserve of food – capital – must be available – enough not only to feed the employees but to tempt them to seek employment.

Now even a neolithic farming household can produce a surplus of food above what its members consume, but some enticement or compulsion is needed to secure the regular production of such a surplus. If enough families live together in the same village the total surplus produced by all, if it be pooled or concentrated, might suffice to support one or two 'non-productive' – i.e. not food-producing – families. Neolithic villages among the forests of temperate Europe were hardly big enough even for this. But irrigation farming in the Near East was more productive, and permitted, indeed encouraged a larger aggregation of farmers. Even pre-pottery neolithic Jericho or Jarmo could have afforded to support a smith; probably they chose to support a professional priest instead. But no more than in Europe could such oasis villages guarantee livelihoods to the large personnel needed to keep a smith supplied with raw material; they could not constitute a reliable market that promised adequate recompense for the exacting toil and frightful risks involved in the extraction, distribution, and processing of metal. To induce, and even to enable, a sufficient number of persons to face these privations and overcome the obstacles and embark on the profession of miner, smelter, or merchant, a surplus much larger than any such village alone could produce was essential.

Now in the alluvial valleys of the Nile, the Tigris-Euphrates, and the Indus, the very rivers that watered and fertilized the soil were also moving roads on which even bulky loads, like grain, could be economically transported. In Egypt, in Lower Mesopotamia – Sumer and Akkad – and in the Indus basin the produce of quite large areas was in fact collected in central granaries and thus made available precisely to liberate such full-time specialists from the business of growing or catching their own food. Historically that involved a social revolution in the river valleys, as we shall see forthwith. But once an effective demand and a reliable market had been established and had evoked well-manned mining and smelting undertakings and a regular system for the transportation of their products to the riverine markets, societies living round the lodes or not too far from the caravan routes could also exert a demand. The modest surpluses available, say in Halafian villages in North Syria, were quite insufficient to offer an assured living to miners or metal-merchants, an effective inducement to persuade anyone to go to the Taurus to mine copper for them or to transport it to them. But once, relying on the Sumerian market, miners had started working the Taurus lodes, and once merchants were conveying their winnings to Sumer and Akkad, the distributors could augment their profits by satisfying the feeble demand of such Halafian villages and supply them with some of the copper in return for a part of their surplus or just for their goodwill. In time Europe too would help to supply Oriental demands for raw materials and luxury goods, and neolithic societies there could likewise benefit from an industry established in reliance on Egyptian and Mesopotamian markets.

The decisive event for European prehistory was the Urban Revolution; it was also a liberating event just because it was completed first in the valleys of the Nile, the Tigris-Euphrates, and the Indus.[54] The Revolution was indeed the precondition of all future progress in science and technology; economically it created the first accumulation of the capital requisite for the fuller exploitation of the earth's natural resources and so for Man's emancipation from parasitic dependence on the non-human environment. But thanks to her very backwardness Europe could benefit from the Orient's achievement without paying the full price, could draw upon accumulated capital without accumulating it. For the Urban Revolution created poverty as well as prosperity; the capital required for urbanization, like that used for industrialization in the nineteenth century, was accumulated by the compulsory savings of the masses – and that is just a euphemism for exploitation.

Each little farmer, herdsman, or fisherman in the alluvial river valleys could – barring an 'act of God' – produce enough food to keep himself and his fast-multiplying family, and a little surplus too. None could or would by himself produce enough to guarantee a livelihood for a single specialist craftsman or merchant or prospector. None by himself could thus liberate anyone from the engrossing quest for food so that he could devote his energy, his skill, or his flair to the execution of highly skilled operations, to the perfecting of techniques, to the discovery of fresh resources, or to the conveyance of raw materials from their remote sources to the inhabited valleys where they were wanted. The use of copper – and *a fortiori* of bronze – demanded all that. On the other hand the tiny surpluses produced by thousands of such peasants would and did suffice to support a staff of specialist craftsmen, miners, and transport workers, perfectly adequate to supply the needs of the primary producers, provided they were pooled or concentrated. And concentrated they were. The cultivators of the alluvial river valleys willingly handed them over to an incarnate god or the representatives of an imaginary deity. Unimpeachable archaeological testimony to this concentration is afforded by the mastaba and pyramid tombs of Egypt, by the monumental temples of Protoliterate Sumer, by the impregnable brick citadels of Harappa and Mohenjo-daro in the Indus basin.

The rare mastaba tombs, still crammed with remains of extravagant luxury, despite early violation by tomb-robbers, and surrounded by the simple graves of servants and retainers, stand out in the sharpest contrast to the countless pit graves in which Egyptian peasants had been and still were interred with modest furniture. The contrast would reveal, patently enough, the elevation of a divine king and a few chosen nobles above the masses even if no written texts survived to record it. Similarly the magnitude of a Sumerian temple and its ornate architecture when compared with any contemporary domestic building is the concrete reflection of the pre-eminence of the god's household in the urban economy that is implied in a great series of archaic accounts, inscribed on clay tablets recovered at the ancient Lagash. The Indus citadels, containing or commanding vast granaries, document the concentration still more explicitly, even though here no decipherable writings disclose the precise source of the rulers' authority. At the same time the extravagant number of metal tools from early pharaohs' tombs, from at least Early Dynastic Sumerian graves, and from the Indus cities provide an economic justification for this concentration. It did in fact form the foundation for a metallurgical industry.

Of course that was not the conscious purpose of the concentration or even the principal use made of the concentrate. Neither were so utilitarian nor so rational – on current standards. Most of the surplus was squandered on unproductive luxuries or futile ceremonials. Thousands of jars of grain and precious alabaster vases were buried in a dead pharaoh's tomb; gallons of beer were brewed daily to invigorate a Sumerian idol. None the less enough was left to pay for the importation of raw materials for industry and for some-reproductive works like canals.

Of course, too, the Urban Revolution was not a single event any more than the Industrial Revolution. It was rather a critical point in a really continuous process. But in Egypt this critical point coincides with a known historical event – the military conquest of the Nile valley from the First Cataract to the Mediterranean coast by the leader of the Falcon clan from Upper Egypt.[55] In prehistoric times the Nile valley seems to have been occupied by a series of totemic clans, each occupying a definite tract along the river. The totem, or mythical ancestor of a clan, in historical times became the emblem of the territory – termed a *nome* by the Greeks – which that clan had occupied. Some figured documents – ivory knife-handles, slate palettes – pictorially record incidents in the struggles of these clans and eventually the triumph of the Falcon clan, with which the preliterate predynastic age ended. In the earlier pictures the actors are exclusively animals; in the latest significant innovations have been introduced. In the 'Lion Hunt palette' the story is still related in mythological form: the enemy is a lion, and his defeat is his slaughter by the

83

victorious hunters. But the victors are men, though they are still led by the clan emblem, the Falcon Horus perched on a standard, not by its incarnation. (*Horus* is just (the latinized form of) the Egyptian word for 'falcon'.) In the culminating scene, 'the Narmer palette', the divine Falcon has become incarnate in a human vehicle; the clan's leader has been identified with the clan's totem and become a divine king. He is portrayed – on this palette is carved the oldest real portrait of a human personality – in supernatural size, twice as big as the attendant who walks behind him. Above him his name is written pictographically like a rebus, enclosed in a simplified representation of his palace's façade surmounted by the Falcon. The inscription, the oldest surviving in the Nile valley, thus reads 'the Horus Narmer'. It asserts and magically maintains the king's identity with the Falcon god.

These pictures not only record historical events; they vividly reflect the social and conceptual transformations that accompanied the economic revolution. At first the actors had been animals, clan totems, symbolizing undivided social groups. Very likely each clan acknowledged a human chief, leader in war and in ritual, but he, too, had been a clansman, followed by fellow clansmen and himself following the totem as much as they. On the Narmer palette the leader, Nar-mer, is no longer a follower of Horus, he is Horus. By their very victory the Falcon clansmen have become his subjects as much as the defeated followers of other totems. A new human institution has emerged. An individual has arisen from society and been enthroned above society: he is a king; he is a god!

The transformation is equally well, its implications even better, illustrated in the funerary record. From the earliest neolithic times the Egyptians had been preoccupied with securing a good burial. Prehistoric burials are all of the

84

same kind, though in the later ones differences in the amount of funerary furniture may reflect differences of wealth. But all the graves were essentially just pits dug in the sand; their uniformity merely reflects the social homogeneity of the clan – or whatever group it was – that used the cemetery. After the union of the two lands, the final unification of Egypt under Narmer's successor, Aha (Menes),[56] side by side with the older pit graves appears a new type of tomb, reserved at first for chiefs of the Falcon clan who have become kings or pharaohs. At their home town and first capital, Abydos, Aha and his successors were each interred at the bottom of a great shaft in a timbered mortuary house that may be a copy of the palace in which he had lived; the shaft was probably surmounted by a square mound or small pyramid of mud brick.[57] Each had a second tomb at Saqqara on the edge of the desert platform overlooking Memphis, the new capital at the apex of the Delta founded by Aha – Menes. Here the grave shaft was surmounted with a more monumental and ornate superstructure, enclosing the square mound of the south and nowadays termed a *mastaba*. This overground monument, that might measure as much as 127 feet in length, 56 feet in breadth, and 30 feet in height,[58] served both as a storehouse for mortuary provisions and as a chapel for the cult of the divine dead; it stood in a walled enclosure or temenos that was planted with trees. The number and costliness of the grave-goods deposited in the royal burial chambers and the superimposed mastabas exceed in numbers and in value those ever deposited with a predynastic corpse or with any ordinary corpse of pharaonic times by so much that the quantitative difference has become a veritably qualitative contrast. In fact the early pharaohs' burials were associated with offerings of a quite novel kind – with human sacrifices. Their tombs at Abydos and at Saqqara are surrounded with rows of little graves, each containing a single contracted skeleton. The furniture of these graves is as poor as that of a predynastic grave, but gives an indication of the deceased's profession in life – cook, barber, coppersmith, lapidary, carpenter, and – once – clerk. The poor little skeletons are obviously those of servants and attendants of the dead king, presumably slain and certainly buried with him to serve him in his sepulchral life. (Under Dynasty II the Egyptians discovered magical ways of animating statues and endowing pictures of tools with all the efficacy of metal ones, and so need no longer bury even with their kings goods so precious as skilled craftsmen and copper saws!)

The contrast between the royal tombs and all previous or contemporary burials in Egypt reveals explicitly the elevation of their occupants above the rest of Egyptian society; the fantastic wealth of foodstuffs, manufactured goods, and imported materials demonstrates the concentration of the valley's wealth in the possession of the pharaoh. The articles made from exotic materials, including heaps of copper chisels, saws, knives, and weapons, suffice to prove that some of this wealth had been expended on the extraction and importation of substances not available in the narrow valley. The manufactured articles – vases of stone and metal, jewellery, richly carved furniture, arms and weapons of copper – are surely the produce of a little army of expert craftsmen who devoted their whole time to the manufacture of works of art, drawing supplies of food and other necessaries directly or indirectly from the royal stores; the artisans buried along with the pharaoh just confirm this inference. But they justify another: the elevation of the Falcon chief to the rank of divine king and the concomitant concentration in his hands of the surplus produce of all the fertile soil irrigated by the Nile had indeed guaranteed craftsmen the opportunity to exercise and perfect their skills without worrying about the production of their food and had secured them regular supplies of the raw materials they needed. But it had not freed them from dependence on Society. On the contrary craftsmen, just like other clansmen, had become subjects of a king who stood above Society while embodying all its compulsive powers.

That is indeed not quite the whole story. Burial under a mastaba, accompanied by human victims, was not strictly confined to pharaohs. Even under the First Dynasty we know some mastaba tombs[59] whose occupants had not attained quite that exalted status. Presumably they were royal officials and provincial governors; for later comparable tombs contain inscriptions indicating that their owners had played just such rôles in the Egyptian State organization. Incidentally they reveal that the privilege of such a burial had been specially conferred by the pharaoh.[55] Perhaps these officers or their ancestors had been, like the pharaoh's own progenitors, clan chiefs who had made timely submission to the conquering Falcon clan. As the chief of the latter clan had been elevated above his fellow-clansmen as well as above the defeated clansmen, so the victor had raised obedient chiefs above their fellow-clansmen, but not of course to the unique eminence of the pharaoh himself. The nobility thus recruited did constitute a ruling class, raised above and contrasted with the mass of the population, but owing this elevation exclusively to the pharaoh and thus – at least in theory – totally dependent on him. In the resultant division of society into classes, into rulers and subjects, the new population of specialist craftsmen was relegated along with the peasantry to the lower class of subjects. Only the clerks (scribes) together with an older group of specialists in magic and cult (priests) succeeded in retaining or attaining an intermediate position,

. dependent indeed on the king and the nobles, but, so long
as they carried out their will, raised above the masses.
Theirs was 'the right to command', but only in so far as
they were the mouthpieces and executants for the ruling
class. The status of clerks and artisans alike is clarified by
burials of both in poor graves round the royal tombs.

In Mesopotamia the mechanism of accumulation appears
to have been more spiritual, and the critical point is less
easily defined than in Egypt. The Revolution was accomplished before even Southern Mesopotamia, before even
its southernmost tract, Sumer, had been united by military
conquests into a single monarchical State or Empire. That
had been first effectively achieved when the city of Agade
or Akkad under its ruler, Sargon, conquered and subjugated the rest of the cities in Lower Mesopotamia. But by
2500 B.C. a score of these, most of them in Sumer, had
already attained full urban status as politically independent
City-States. Moreover, the surplus produce of the peasantry
was concentrated first in the temples of imaginary deities,
not in the granaries of a conquering monarch.

Prehistoric Halafian and 'Ubaid communities even in
Northern Mesopotamia, unlike neolithic villages in Temperate Europe and Greece, had been populous enough, and
therefore produced enough surplus food, to build relatively
luxurious houses for their deities and probably enough to
support specialist priests to serve them. The colonists of the
delta land of Sumer, thriving on irrigation cultivation,
maintained the same religious traditions and built still finer
houses for their gods or goddesses. These were repeatedly
reconstructed on an ever grander scale on the same
hallowed site at the centre of the settlement. So each site
became a tell, a mound composed of the debris of successive
and superimposed villages and cities. The excavation, layer
by layer, of such tells – Eridu, Erech (Warka), Lagash

(Tello), Ur – has concretely revealed the growth of the temple step by step from a modest 'neolithic' shrine measuring perhaps 10 by 9 feet in area to a monumental fane attaining such dimensions as 220 by 95 feet. The growth in size alone – it was actually accompanied by a parallel enrichment of decorative architecture and furniture –symbolizes and measures the growing wealth of the temple's divine owner, accumulated as 'first-fruits' and 'tithes' from the surplus produced by 'the god's people'. The process is so finely divided in the successive building-levels that it seems arbitrary to fix the exact critical point at which quantity passed over into quality, when the Revolution was accomplished. It is conventionally fixed at what is called the Late Uruk or Protoliterate Period when the first – still undecipherable – written documents appear.

When a little later, in Early Dynastic II or III to use archaeological terminology, decipherable texts become available, we find the temples each organized as a sort of divine household,[60] gods own the city's land which they are reputed to have created, though it was really created by the citizens' own labour in digging channels to drain swamps and convey water to sandy desert. Part of each god's land is parcelled out among his people, who owe him rent in kind and labour services. Part is exploited as the god's personal demesne by these tenants or wage-labourers. The surplus, thus extracted, serves not only to provide the god with enormous feasts, but also to pay for the importation of raw materials – metals, timber, stone – not available on the alluvial plain, and to feed specialist craftsmen who may also have held lots in the temple lands. Thus a new industrial population was guaranteed a livelihood and supplied with raw materials. In addition the god was served by equally specialist priests who now came to form hierarchical corporations. They alone could interpret the god's will and organize its fulfilment. They took over the administration of the god's estate and the direction of his people. Naturally they too were paid for their services, i.e. supported from the temple's store. Indeed they were well paid. One high temple official at Lagash held a lot of 35.5 acres, fourteen times as big as the normal holding of a citizen.[61] Indeed we read of exactions – excessive fees demanded for burials, appropriation for private use of the god's demesne land, improper eviction of humble tenants.[62]

The god's self-appointed ministers had taken over from the masses the direction of the divine household. They monopolized the mystery of writing which they had invented in order to keep the god's accounts. The new craftsmen on the other hand acquired security, regular supplies of raw materials and the opportunity to devote their lives to the exercise of their peculiar skills at the price of attachment to the divine estate and subjection to its priestly administrators. Still, in the Protoliterate Period a Sumerian Temple State may have been more like an enormously enlarged patriarchal family than a class society. The priesthood in so far as it monopolized directive functions, could be termed a ruling class. But its members remained the god's servants, as much as peasants and artisans, and administered his estate on his behalf, not for private gain.

By Early Dynastic II, however, the oldest texts that we can read already mention a 'city king', generally styled *ishakku*, 'tenant farmer (of the god)', rarely *lugal*, 'lord'.[63] He, on behalf of the god, led the citizens in war against neighbouring cities; he acted perhaps as the god's incarnation in fertility rites and was sometimes at least high priest of the principal god. In that capacity, at least in Lagash,[60] the *ishakku* had sole control of the city's granaries. In theory a city king was as much a servant of the god as any other citizen – priest, artisan, or farmer – and therefore not qualitatively differentiated from the rest of the citizen body. But if not already raised by economic power (control of the food reserves) or by ritual identification with the deity above society like a pharaoh, the city king might reach the same sort of eminence by the same road. Towards the close of Early Dynastic III, about 2400 B.C., Entemena of Lagash, then Lugalzaggisi of Erech, and finally Sargon of Agade, had led their citizen armies to the conquest of other cities and had so become masters, no longer fellow-servants, of defeated populations. As in Egypt, these victories may have entailed the subjection of the victorious citizens, too. Though the above-mentioned conquests are the first that are documented by contemporary inscriptions and Sargon's the first known to have outlasted the conqueror's reign, they were not demonstrably unprecedented. On the contrary, later Sumerian historians believed that rulers of one city or another had exercised lordship over all the rest from a remote 'antediluvian' epoch. They composed a list of cities and kings that had thus ruled over the whole land, beginning with eight 'antediluvian' dynasties and recommencing 'after the Flood' with a 'First Dynasty of Kish'.[64]

Now from Early Dynastic I (3175 and 2675 B.C. seem equally well justified guesses at a date for its beginning) archaeology discloses palaces, as well as temples, and graves deserving the epithet 'royal' at Kish, Ur, Mari, and at Susa in Elam. In contrast to the simple trenches in which ordinary citizens were interred from the neolithic age throughout historical times, these quite exceptional 'royal tombs' are large subterranean chambers, each containing besides the principal corpse the bodies of two or more attendants, a wheeled vehicle used as a hearse together with draft oxen or asses (onagers) and an extravagantly rich furniture. Though far from matching in monumental grandeur and lavishness of grave-goods the mastaba tombs of the pharaohs in Egypt, they must yet belong to persons raised above the rest of their societies. In Mesopotamia, as in Egypt, the Urban Revolution was at least quickly followed by the emergence out of Society of a king, raised above it and thus enabled, more effectively than a barbarian chief or an imaginary deity, to concentrate a social surplus. Indeed in Mesopotamia too, the emergence of kingship may actually coincide with the critical point in the process of accumulation. It has been plausibly contended[65] that the burst of building that marks the beginning of the Proto-literate Period at Erech reflects that city's rise to imperial status under the dynasty of the legendary Gilgamesh, the First Dynasty of Erech in the Sumerian king-list; scenes of battle and bound captives are in fact conspicuous on seals of that period. In that case the capital for the completion of the Urban Revolution would have been derived from the spoils of war supplementing the tithes and other offerings peacefully accumulated in Sumerian temples. It is equally arguable that the critical point has been wrongly assessed; the abundance of metal tools, arms, vessels, and ornaments that should signalize the regular establishment of a metal-lurgical industry has not actually been found before Early Dynastic I (but perhaps just because no Protoliterate ceme-teries have been excavated). In either case it is still very possible that in Mesopotamia, as in Egypt, the capital to complete the Urban Revolution was accumulated by a divine king, raised to a godlike eminence above Society.

Be that as it may, Sargon of Agade and his successors, though never so divine as a pharaoh nor so rich, did come to personify a State raised above Society. Though not quite equal to the older gods and goddesses, Mesopotamian kings were deified. The temples depended for embellish-ment, enlargement, and even repair upon the court. No Mesopotamian kingdom was so totalitarian as the Egyptian.[66] Still the Babylonian king was far and away the largest purchaser of imported materials, of manufactured goods, and of craftsmanship. The metal trade was at times a royal monopoly; merchants emphasize their dependence on the monarch in their letters, signing themselves 'servant of the king of X'.[67]

Thus in Egypt divine kings, in Mesopotamia deities and city-kings accumulated reserves ample enough to support a new population of full-time specialists and to guarantee to professional craftsmen security to exercise and perfect their skills. It further supported, directly or indirectly, those engaged in the extraction and transportation of raw materials required in industry; Egypt and Mesopotamia both lacked metals and building timber, Mesopotamia stone too, and both came to demand what we might call luxuries – lapis lazuli and other semi-precious stones, fragrant woods, wine, olive oil – that must also be imported. Thanks to the trade thus financed by the new States, Egyptian and Sumerian craftsmen were also supplied regularly with materials on which to exercise their crafts. So the Urban Revolution fulfilled the prerequisites of a Bronze Age: it liberated artisans from the necessity of growing or catching their own food so that they might devote their whole time to industry and it insured them regular supplies of metal. But it reduced the very craftsmen whom it had liberated to economic servitude; they were utterly dependent on the State both for their food and for their raw materials. They were proletarians, who must earn their living by selling their labour or their skill.

The ideological consequences of the class division are no less significant than its economic foundations. In simple societies, not yet divided into classes, practical life, including the application of science, is guided by Custom, and Custom no doubt embodies the society's collective experience,

the wisdom gathered and tested by ancestral generations, the science of the period. No doubt too the
interpretation of Custom, the application of traditional
rules of behaviour to specific cases, was left to Old Men or
to chiefs. But both were just the repositories of Custom,
not its creators. In so far as they modified customary practice, they were guided by their own experience and that of
fellow-tribesmen or clansmen. The procedure was frus-
tratingly slow and might be hopelessly obstructive, but it
was in a real sense democratic or popular.

All this was changed by the Urban Revolution. Custom,
the unconscious creation of Society, is replaced by laws and
regulations imposed on Society by – or in the name of –
gods above and outside Society. Their interpretation is
entrusted to a divine king who himself establishes laws as
his decrees or to a corporation of priests to whom the gods'
wills are exclusively revealed. Conformity can be enforced
by the unique economic power concentrated in the hands
of a divine king or of a kingly god whose exclusive control
of society's food reserves is backed up by a virtual monopoly of metal armaments and, in Mesopotamia, of chariotry
too. The masses surrendered the right and duty of fore-
thought and planning to deities or devotees and, relieved
of the embarrassments of decision, accepted irresponsible
obedience. No doubt the new rulers could plan more
wisely and so more successfully than a council of village
elders or a clan chief. They had invented scripts, devices for
recording in conventional symbols their observations and
thus transmitting the collective experience more fully and
more accurately than can be done by memory alone. By
the same token they had devised conventional systems of
numeral notation that facilitated and ultimately trans-
formed the operation of counting. And, having standardized measurement, they were enabled to quantify some

realms of experience. For example, the pharaoh's ministers were able to tell the Egyptian peasants when to start the annual cycle of agricultural operations; for they had measured the tropic year and established a scientific calendar. Similarly Sumerian temple officers could predict correctly the quantity of seed needed to sow a given field.

The peasant masses did really benefit by surrendering responsibility and the burden of decision to the godlike State if only because State planning was to some extent based on a rudimentary exact science. The trouble was that too little of the practical lore of the peasantry and less of that of the new crafts was incorporated and systematized in the new recorded knowledge. For writing was a mystery and the few initiates, if not actually rulers, were at least raised above the subject masses. 'You hold the pen. It is yours to command. The clerk is exempt from all manual tasks,' runs a rather late Egyptian text.[68] It may well exaggerate the dignity enjoyed by scribes, but certainly reflects the ambitions of the clerical bureaucracy. The reaction of this class division on technical and scientific progress in the Orient was disastrous. Progress demands not only new inventions, but also fresh needs for these to satisfy; an invention for which there is no effective demand cannot itself be effective. Now a prehistoric metal-worker presumably would have no difficulty in persuading of the superiority of metal weapons or tools his fellow-clansmen or his war-chief, who would have to use them. It would be quite another matter to convince a divine king whose active participation in combat is enormously exaggerated in his monuments, while clerks wielding pens would not be interested in saws or sickles. At the same time the peasantry were so thoroughly stripped of surplus produce, that is, of purchasing power, that they could not afford metal tools; such were indeed available in a Sumerian temple's store, but in Egypt even in nobles' tombs the workers on the owner's estate are shown reaping with flint-armed wooden sickles. So the new craftsmen, relegated to the lower classes and thereby relieved of responsibility for decision, were at the same time deprived of a market for labour-saving devices and so of all stimulus to fresh inventions. So in Egypt and Mesopotamia the simple types of axe, adze, knife, dagger, and spear, perfected about 3000 B.C., survived with little change during the next two millennia; in a celebrated tomb picture native Egyptian smiths about 400 B.C. are depicted using the same[69] inefficient equipment as in similar pictures of the Pyramid Age 2,000 years earlier.

Finally, the relegation of craftsmen to the lower class excluded them from literacy and isolated the pure sciences of Egyptian and Sumerian clerks from the applied sciences of miners, smelters, smiths, and potters. Craft lore could not be committed to writing but continued to be handed on by precept and example. Just for this reason it remained empirical and particular while learned science was not fertilized by experience gained in workshop practice. Yet we repeat, European science owes more to the lore of illiterate artisans than to the speculations of learned clerks. In brief, the Urban Revolution in Egypt and Mesopotamia had liberated craftsmen from the food quest only to consign them to an exploited subject class; it supplied them with raw materials on which to exercise their skills, but no inducement to improve them; it guaranteed them security of employment, but no prospect of a superior status. That was the consequence of the cleavage of society into classes and the exploitation of the masses by a narrow ruling class. This class division and exploitation were historically necessary to amass the resources and evoke the personnel required to get a bronze industry established. But when it had been established by that division of Egyptian and Mesopotamian societies, other communities could utilize that machinery without themselves submitting to the same degree of exploitation.

Most of the communities in South-west Asia in a position to profit from the extractive and distributive organization thus created, though they had not had to accumulate the resources themselves, were sooner or later – but generally sooner – split up into classes. Some were forcibly urbanized by military conquest; for Sargon of Agade had initiated a policy of aggressive imperialism aiming at securing in the form of booty or tribute the raw materials needed by Mesopotamian industry; his armies drove to the Levant coasts and the Taurus to lay hands on the forests and lodes of ore. Though his empire was ephemeral, he was quickly imitated by other Mesopotamian monarchs. To resist imperialist aggression its potential victims must build up an army and equip it with costly metal armaments and still more costly war-chariots. The victorious resistance leader could easily turn into a king. A barbarian chief, as the richest tribesman, could most readily acquire the requisite armaments, and they could be used against rebels as well as against aggressors. In other communities local chiefs by presents or bribes from prospectors and merchants were rendered economically independent of the customary gifts, traditionally due from fellow-tribesmen. So they could ape the pharaohs or the kings of Kish. So by 2000 B.C. Palestine, Syria, the Levant Coasts were dotted with petty kingdoms, each replicating more or less the class structure of Egyptian and Sumerian States. And there, of course, even neolithic communities had been populous enough to afford professional priests. These could now elucubrate an ideology to sanctify and legitimize the authority of the new kings.

European societies were too remote to be exposed to

imperialist attacks. They were too small and poor to afford professional priests or chiefs so exalted that they might aspire to kingly status. Yet they were not too remote to reach the Oriental markets or too poor to supply their demands. So they could benefit by the machinery created by the Urban Revolution, but postpone the class division it entailed till the new professional craftsmen had won for themselves a status they never acquired in the Ancient East.

CHAPTER 7

THE EARLY BRONZE AGE IN THE MEDITERRANEAN

(i) THE EARLY AEGEAN CYCLE

THE first Europeans to draw, directly or indirectly, on the accumulated wealth of Oriental civilization were the populations of the Aegean coasts and islands. By legitimate commerce they supplied Egyptian and Mesopotamian demands for raw materials that they themselves could produce or at least transport in their ships. They could also raid the Nile Delta and secondary centres of urban life on the Levant coasts; commerce and piracy were always closely interwoven in the Mediterranean world, and the story of a raid on the Delta after the Trojan War, told by Odysseus in Homer's *Odyssey*, though admittedly fictitious, was intended to sound plausible. Thus by peaceful trade or naked force Aegean peoples did obtain a share in the Oriental surplus. They used it to develop a genuinely European bronze industry.

All the populations concerned were closely related in that they shared distinctive common traditions, particularly in pottery and architecture. So they are figured in the archaeological record by a single culture-cycle, the Early Aegean. This does not mean that they were genetically akin or racially homogeneous. The Early Aegean culture-cycle embraces five or six cultures which, despite many common traits, can easily be distinguished and most of which can be further subdivided: what we shall call Early Troadic culture embraced not only the Troad and its Asiatic hinterland as far as Mysia, but at least the adjacent islands of Lesbos and Lemnos and Gallipoli on the European side of

99

the Dardanelles. The Early Thracic culture of the Maritza valley (known today from one site only, Mikhalic) and the Early Macednic, in Macedonia and inland Thessaly, are culturally as well as geographically intermediate between Early Troadic and Early Helladic. The latter ruled on coastal Thessaly, Central Greece, Attica, and the Peloponnese, and spread westward along the Gulf of Corinth to Levkas and Ithaka. The island belt was occupied by the Early Cycladic culture, while Crete had her own Early Minoan culture with Egyptian as well as Cycladic and Asiatic affinities. Finally on Cyprus, the Copper Island, despite marked peculiarities conformable to the island's geographical position, Early Cypriote culture[70] is more closely allied to those of the Aegean proper than to any yet known on the nearer coasts of Hither Asia.

All these regions, save for the smaller islands, had already been occupied in neolithic times. Many Early Aegean settlements had indeed been the sites of neolithic villages, but some were explicitly new foundations. Divergent neolithic traditions had doubtless been carried over into the Bronze Age and may help to account for some of the differences observed between the several Early Aegean cultures. Yet no culture of the Early Aegean cycle is simply derivable from any one known neolithic culture of the region. On the contrary the peculiar innovations, common to all Early Aegean cultures, give the impression that all were due to a fresh colonization. Nevertheless, no single culture is known outside the Aegean area that exhibits all the novelties in embryo. Let us admit that the Early Aegean cultures developed where we find them, leaving aside as at present unanswerable and perhaps illegitimate the question whence the responsible populations came. For the Early Aegean cycle was fundamentally a maritime one; the community of traditions it expresses was based on, and maintained by, the frequent and indeed regular interchange of goods (actually recorded archaeologically) and of persons and ideas (inferred therefrom) between coastal settlements all round the Aegean and on the islands that bridge that sea. And it was by seaways that Aegean merchants tapped the markets of Egypt and the Levant and secured resources for the development of handicraft and commerce. Inland settlements, in Arcadia or Boeotia for example, were comparatively poor just because their contacts with the Orient were at second hand through the coastal townships.

Early Aegean settlements, save Early Thracic and Early Macednic, appear as complexes of rooms with stone foundations grouped along narrow tortuous alleys. The number of distinct houses is uncertain, but the occupied areas were absurdly small – Troy I, 1·25 acres, Troy II, less than two acres, Phylakopi on Melos somewhat more than four acres. But all sites were continuously occupied over a long period so that their ruins form tells whose stratigraphical excavation provides a basis for the relative chronology of Aegean prehistory. Five superimposed 'cities' at Troy are assigned to the Early Aegean period, and all 'cities' – but particularly I and II – underwent several phases of drastic rebuilding. Five architectural periods were recognized at Thermi on Lesbos, but these were contemporary only with Troy I and early Troy II. Stratigraphy and typology justify a division of Early Minoan into three phases – E.M. I, II, and III – and similar divisions have been proposed for Early Helladic (E.H.), Early Cycladic (E.C.), and Early Cypriote. The end of the Early Aegean period is conventionally put at 1800 B.C. in Greece and the Troad, nearer 2100 in Crete. Its commencement is still a matter of guessing, but E.M. I may begin as early as the Urban Revolution in Egypt, about 3000 B.C.

Most of the inhabitants of the coastal townships must

have been farmers, securing their own food by cultivation, stock-breeding, and fishing. Inland settlements in Central Greece, Macedonia, and Thrace were quite simply peasant villages. Everywhere, however, the farmers must have cultivated vines and fruit-trees in addition to cereals and vegetables. And all Early Aegean farmers had almost certainly advanced from plot-cultivation with hoes to the tillage of fields with ox-drawn ploughs; ploughing is actually represented in a model from an Early Cypriote tomb.[71] On the other hand the tiny island of Pseira off Crete was occupied by a community that must have lived on maritime commerce; for the islet is too small for farming, but boasts an excellent spring. Some of the smaller Cyclades too may well have relied on imported food.

In any case in all coastal settlements farming was combined with handicrafts and commerce, and professional craftsmen and traders lived among the peasants. The potters' craft indeed was not yet mechanized anywhere in Europe, but at Troy some families of professional potters arrived and set up their wheels during the lifetime of Troy II; during the rest of the Early Troadic period their mass-produced wares copied, and competed with, the products of older domestic industry. In Crete, too, lived families of potters, specialized enough to need private seals. But these did not yet use the wheel and may well have been itinerants, not residing in, or relying on the surplus produced by, a single village, but perambulating the island as groups of potters do today.[72]

Smiths must have been resident in all the larger townships, and they were surely full-time specialists. In most places their raw material would have to be imported. Of copper ores there are, of course, rich lodes in Cyprus and smaller deposits in Naxos, in Crete and elsewhere. On the north-east coasts of Attica at Rafina, a refinery has recently been excavated whither copper ore was shipped, perhaps from Naxos, to be smelted with charcoal from the adjacent forests clothing the slopes of Pentelicus and Hymettus. But even in Early Aegean times the copper was often alloyed with tin to make bronze. The oldest known object of metallic tin is a bracelet from Thermi, and standard bronze, containing 10 per cent tin, is illustrated by chisels from Troy II. Lead, silver, and gold were also used and at Troy and in Crete were doubtless worked by professional jewellers.

Beads of hard stone, particularly in Crete, vases of alabaster on the Cyclades and of variegated stones in Crete should likewise rank as products of specialists. And so should finely engraved seals in Crete. The designs are often the instruments or operations of craftsmen, as in Proto-literate Mesopotamia, and reveal the existence of other professionals – potters, carpenters, merchants, and boat-builders. The sea-going ships, depicted on Early Minoan seals and on Cycladic and Helladic vases, must have been at least designed by professional shipwrights; they might attain a length of 50 feet and were propelled by many rowers; sails are not represented before the Middle Minoan period.

The professional craftsmen who first manufactured most of the foregoing commodities were doubtless either immigrants from the Orient or had served apprenticeship to such. The potters' wheel, for instance, invented in Proto-literate Sumer, was presumably diffused by younger children or apprentices of Sumerian potters, migrating as the local markets became overcrowded, till after many generations a few found patrons at Troy. At Troy, too, goldsmiths reproduced highly specialized traditional types that their fellow-craftsmen made in the same traditional way on the Anatolian plateau and on the banks of the Nile, the Euphrates, and even the Indus. But while sometimes thus betraying the sources of their skills, craftsmen in the Aegean did not go on just repeating Egyptian or Asiatic models, but adapted their output to local tastes. Moreover the original immigrants had not all belonged to one and the same school. In metal work Egyptian as well as Meso-potamian traditions are discernible. Thus arose original Aegean schools of metallurgy and other arts blending diverse foreign traditions; native-born descendants or apprentices of immigrants manufactured distinctively Aegean types to cater for local tastes and local habits of working or fighting.

Whether or no merchants were professionals, trade within the Aegean area is abundantly documented by the distribu-tion of raw materials and manufactures. Obsidian, for instance, from the volcanic islands of Melos and Yali was transported all over the Aegean and well into the hinter-land; much was exported from Melos in the form of blades struck on the island from ingeniously prepared cores. The sources of copper have already been mentioned. Silver could have been obtained from the famous deposits of Laurion in Attica as well as from Asia Minor. Among manufactures of definite provenance we may mention vases and figurines of Cycladic marble which reached the Troad, the Peloponnese, and Crete. Even pots were trans-ported quite long distances and naturally not empty but filled with luxury foods, unguents, or spices. So fragments of Early Helladic vases, made in Mainland Greece, turned up in all the 'cities' of Troy save 'early 1'. Conversely, vessels of Troadic form or fabric have been recognized in Thrace, on Euboea, and in Central Greece. Again, sealings from jars or bales of merchandise, stamped in Crete with Early Minoan seals, were recovered from the Early Helladic settlement at Asine on the east coast of the Peloponnese.

The Early Aegean Cycle

Archaeological evidence for Aegean traffic with those Oriental markets, reliance on which is supposed here to have evoked all the commercial activity just mentioned, is frankly exiguous. Actual manufactures, imported from the Orient into the Aegean world, are virtually limited to a few Asiatic cylinder seals and Egyptian stone vases found stray in Crete. Nor have many Early Aegean manufactures survived in the Near East; a vase of Cycladic marble in a Predynastic Egyptian grave is the best attested. Most of the exports in return for which Aegean peoples secured a share in the Oriental surplus must have been raw materials or perishable luxuries, like oil, wines, unguents, and textiles. Aegean communities were in a position to supply building timber, copper, lead, silver, obsidian, marble, and emery; emery, reputedly from Naxos, did actually reach the Nile in Predynastic times, while Cretan textiles are mentioned in Mesopotamian documents, though not before 2000 B.C.

Still, Aegean exports were not necessarily confined to local products. Tin seems to have been relatively more common in the Aegean than anywhere in South-west Asia or Egypt between 3000 and 2000 B.C. Now tin is a comparatively rare metal; no significant deposits have been identified in Hither Asia or North Africa; Greece itself on geological grounds is a most unpromising area.[73] But Central and Western Europe do possess rich ores. If Aegean peoples before 2000 B.C. were drawing on these supplies, as they demonstrably were doing after 1500, they would have had a vital commodity to offer on the Oriental markets. The ambiguous evidence for Early Aegean voyaging in the west will be discussed in the next section. Luxury articles at least Aegean peoples did obtain by long distance 'trade'. A vase made of liparite, a variegated stone imported from the Aeolian Islands, was found in Crete;[74] beads of possibly Baltic amber and of lapis lazuli from

Afghanistan were included in the treasures of Troy II. So Early Aegean communities were already rich enough to be secondary centres of demand and markets for barbarian European products.

Most Aegean communities exhibit to archaeologists war-like characters. Weapons are very conspicuous in Early Cycladic graves and are relatively common on settlement sites elsewhere. Troy, Poliochni on Lemnos, and coastal sites in Mainland Greece were strongly fortified, but Thermi on Lesbos, Phylakopi on Melos, and all known Minoan sites did without artificial defences in Early Aegean times. The frequent conflicts implied by these walls and weapons did not result in the establishment of any permanent empire such as had been achieved by Entemena or Sargon in the Tigris-Euphrates valley. For a brief time indeed Troy may have conquered a tiny domain in the north-east corner of the Aegean; Thermi and Poliochni did suffer a sort of eclipse just at the time when Troy II was at the height of its prosperity. But if that prosperity and those townships' decline were the results of successful imperialism, they did not last long. Troy II was sacked and burned, but not before the richer townsfolk had buried a really fantastic amount of gold and silver. Their hidden treasures remained concealed till Heinrich Schliemann dug them up in 1873. So it may be inferred that their well-to-do owners perished. Craftsmen and other humbler folk survived. In the succeeding townships, Troy III to V, the distinctive local traditions in architecture and pottery were maintained by descendants of the vanquished population, and developed beyond the point attained before the sack.

So no Early Aegean war-chief could have attained to kingship as the master of a conquered population. Chiefs were indeed acknowledged at Troy, where a palatial hall dominated the citadels of the first and second 'cities', and at

Lerna in the Peloponnese. But the dignitaries thus housed can hardly have been raised above the rest of their communities like a pharaoh or a Sumerian city-king, and surely ruled no subjects in conquered towns. Not even chieftainship of the simple barbarian pattern is attested in other townships. Some inequality in the distribution of wealth is doubtless indicated by the contrast between large and small houses such as has been observed particularly well at Poliochni.[75] It does not amount to a regular class division; there was no 'artisans' quarter' as in Indus cities. Large and small houses were evenly distributed in the town-plan of Poliochni and often closely juxtaposed so that rich and poor mingled easily. In Early Aegean communities neither chiefs nor a small wealthy class alone concentrated a social surplus.

Burial practices suggest an equally simple social structure. On the Asiatic coasts individual burial in cemeteries outside the settlement seems to have been the rule. The cemeteries of Troy I–V, Thermi, and Poliochni have not indeed been discovered, but in the known cemeteries the bodies were enclosed in large jars and accompanied by an even, but rather poor furniture. In Crete, peninsular Greece, Cyprus, and most of the islands collective burial in ossuaries was normal. The ossuaries might be natural caves, rock-cut chambers entered by a stepped pit ('pit caves') or a horizontal or descending passage (Cyprus, Cyclades, Euboea), chambers built in an open excavation lined and covered with dry-stone masonry, corbelling inward to form a roof (Attica, Cyclades), or with slabs on edge (Attica, Cyclades), and bone enclosures, rectangular or circular in plan (Crete), and in the latter case sometimes roofed by corbelling. The built chambers were always provided with an entrance though some at least of the bodies were actually introduced through the roof. Presumably all these types of built tomb imitate traditional homes of the living. The rectangular bone enclosures of Crete exactly reproduce the houses of Early Minoan townships. So the circular ossuaries, termed 'tholoi' by archaeologists, should document round huts, not yet attested by excavation and of African ancestry. Round huts are of course traditional in Africa but were built in Cyprus in neolithic times.

None of these tombs can be compared with the mastabas and pyramids of Egypt. The most monumental are the circular ossuaries of Crete; some have an internal diameter of nearly 40 feet with walls 5 to 8 feet thick that still stand 3 or 4 feet high; but today parties of Cretan shepherds still build beehive-shaped cheese-stores of dry stone that are not much inferior in size to the Early Minoan ossuaries and are built by an identical method. These Early Minoan, like most other Early Aegean, ossuaries are said to have contained a very large number of skeletons, and are shown by their furniture to have been used for burials over a long period. All were in fact 'family vaults' in which deceased members of a kinship group were interred for many generations. Was this group a clan, a lineage, or a 'natural family'? At Krazi in the mountains of Central Crete one small corbelled tholos served as the repository for the bones of the whole community. But on the plain of the Mesara in Southern Crete the great circular ossuaries cluster in groups of three or four. Quite a large cemetery of corbelled and slab-lined chambers surrounds the little township of Hagios Kosmas on the south coast of Attica near the Piraeus. A cemetery of 500 tombs is reported on the island of Syros. At Hagios Kosmas and on the Cyclades the later tombs contain only one skeleton each but in Cyprus it is the earlier tombs that often contain a single burial. In East Crete too some Early Minoan cemeteries consist entirely of single graves, each containing one skeleton enclosed in a pottery jar (pithos), a clay coffin (larnax), or a little box of stone slabs (cist) in the Early Troadic manner.

In none of the Early Aegean cemeteries is any qualitative difference in sepulchral architecture or burial ritual observable, while discrepancies in wealth of furniture do not amount to a disparity of status. The funerary record from the Aegean gives no hint of that division of society that is so patently reflected in the same record on the Nile. A cult of ancestral spirits was no doubt a major factor in maintaining social solidarity. It hardly contributed to the concentration of wealth.

Nor was this effected by imaginary deities, worshipped in temples and served by professional priests. Nothing has been found in the prehistoric Aegean to deserve the name of temple at all. Particularly on Crete natural caves and hill-tops seem to have been frequented as places of cult, but the votive offerings deposited there were mainly cheap statuettes or vases of clay. A clay model from an Early Cypriote tomb[71] represents a sacred enclosure open to the air where rustic rites – dances or ceremonial ploughing – were being celebrated with musical accompaniment. Such sacred places were clearly not suited to the accumulation of valuable offerings or even foodstuffs. Female figurines were still being modelled in clay or carved in stone in Early Aegean settlements as in neolithic villages. Though more conventionalized than their neolithic precursors, they presumably represent the old Mother Goddess. A stele carved with the owl face of a female personage found outside the walls of Troy I, and a few of the marble 'Cycladic idols' alone are large enough to have served as cult statues. But none was found in a temple, and Cycladic idols include, besides females, men and musicians. If the figurines represent the first incarnations of the several Ladies who were patronesses of the various city-states of historical times, none yet boasted a local abode nor had earned a reputation that would bring her worshippers and votaries from outside the local group that had imagined her; none of these local Ladies is yet Athena, Hera, Artemis, or Aphrodite, and we cannot say on which history was to confer that international dignity.

Moreover a Mother Goddess was no longer the sole object of veneration. Some Early Aegean statuettes represent males, and the masculine symbol, the phallus, was also modelled in clay or carved in stone. Such symbols imply the recognition of the father's rôle in procreation, if not the emergence of male deities, and an undermining of the ideological bases of such 'matriarchy' as may be attributed to neolithic communities just at the time when the substitution of ploughs guided by men for hoes wielded by women destroyed its economic foundation.

So between 3000 and 2000 B.C. Aegean societies had succeeded in building up a bronze industry and indeed machinery for the extraction, distribution and processing of other raw materials as well as metals; their economy sufficed to guarantee a living to the requisite personnel. But this they had done without themselves accumulating an enormous surplus and therefore without generating an unbridgeable chasm to divide society irrevocably into opposing classes. Even if we admit a contrast between rich and poor, craftsmen and merchants were not thereby relegated to a subject lower class. No doubt Aegean peoples could achieve this only because the essential reserves had been accumulated and the new techniques and processes discovered and perfected in response to a demand made effective by the class division of Egyptian and Sumerian societies. The establishment of a Bronze Age economy in the Aegean was in fact promoted by Oriental capital as truly as the industrialization of India or Japan in the nineteenth century was effected by British and American capital. But the Aegean had not thereby become a colonial province in an Egyptian or Mesopotamian economic empire.

No doubt the secrets of metallurgy and other techniques had been discovered in the Orient and apparatus for their economical application had been invented there much as the industrial use of coal and steam engines was discovered and invented in north-western Europe. No doubt, too, these discoveries and inventions had been introduced by actual immigrant craftsmen and prospectors. Let us admit that prospectors from the older centres of civilization had discovered the lodes of ore and other raw material whose value had first been appreciated in the Near East. Let us admit that coppersmiths, goldsmiths, seal-engravers, and other artisans had emigrated to the Aegean coasts. In neither case had they arrived as agents of a foreign state or emissaries of alien profit-making concerns. The hypothetical prospectors no doubt would and could have come only because they were assured of a certain market in Egypt or Mesopotamia. Yet they would not and could not ship their winnings exclusively to those markets. In so far as native Aegean communities could contribute to their support, they must first satisfy this local demand; the metal gear from tombs and settlements should show that they did. They must surely have enlisted the help of native workers and thereby initiated such helpers into their technique. After all they were not directing applications of an abstract science, expressed in highly conventionalized mathematical symbols that only the 'educated' could understand; they were themselves executing manual operations that can easily be imitated if not understood. Oriental prospectors could not help initiating Aegean peasants into the practical applications of their lore.

Perhaps they did keep secret the magic rituals that such lore also prescribed, but that was anything but a handicap to the initiates!

Craftsmen, wherever they had come from, were frankly emigrants seeking to find new patrons and to earn a living by supplying the demands of Aegean communities. They certainly brought with them not only abstract skills, but also standardized forms of expressing these, well exemplified in certain complex gold beads that are common to Troy, Central Anatolia, Ur, and Harappa. Still, they were ready to adapt traditional types to local tastes. And they too would accept native apprentices and initiate them into their mysteries. Very few Early Aegean ornaments or weapons, vases or seals are recognizable reproductions of standard Egyptian or Mesopotamian ones; most are novel Aegean types. Indeed in the Aegean world even during the third millennium the variety of distinctive types in metalwork, jewellery, seals, and lapidaries' products is much greater than in Egypt or Mesopotamia during the same period. This originality and willingness to vary traditional models must be partly due to the mere fact of the transplantation of craft traditions to a new social environment. It is no less due to that environment itself and to the position a craftsman or merchant could occupy therein.

Both had, of course, to find a market for their skills or their wares, and patrons to support them. But their clients were relatively far less restricted than in the Ancient East, never limited to a single totalitarian court or an all-embracing divine household. At Troy and Lerna no doubt the best patrons for craftsmen or merchants would be the chiefs whose palaces archaeologists have unearthed. But these were neither emperors, ruling conquered cities, nor divine kings, raised high above their fellows. They would not be exempted from manual labour or active service in war any more than a Maori chief or the headman of a Kayan village in Borneo.[76] Elsewhere perhaps the market for craft skills and imported wares tended to be limited to the more prosperous townsfolk, but these again were practical farmers or navigators who could appreciate labour-saving tools and more efficient weapons.

Moreover the craftsman or merchant could choose his market. There were hundreds of townships and villages round the Aegean – Homer speaks of 'a hundred cities' in Crete albeit a thousand years later– and all seem politically and economically independent. The distances between them were small and intercourse was evidently frequent. Of course travel through mountains and forests where wild beasts still lurked was arduous and perilous. Of course voyaging, even on the Aegean, was far more risky than the modern steamer passenger can dream. Of course 'stranger' is synonymous with 'enemy' in a barbarian society. Yet these obstacles to communications were in fact overcome. So discrimination was possible for craftsmen and merchants.

So Early Aegean craftsmen were producing for an international market and not just to satisfy demands constituted by the traditional tastes and habits of a single society. Each community would develop divergent fashions and working practices. A craftsman should adjust his techniques and his output to the consequent local variations of demand. Thus he was encouraged not merely to maintain a fixed standard of technical competence, but also to excel it, not just to reproduce a fixed range of standard types, but also to introduce innovations that should by their efficiency or beauty attract discriminating purchasers. This stimulus to originality was due precisely to the multiplicity of distinct but intercommunicating societies and to the assumed mobility of the craftsmen among them. The latter assumption cannot indeed be proved archaeologically; it is a fair inference from the conditions of Homeric and Classical Greece.[77] Homer declares that 'a craftsman is welcome everywhere' and relates how Tychios was summoned from Boeotia to make a shield for Ajax in Locris. In the fifth century a high proportion of the merchants and craftsmen operating in Athens were resident aliens (*metics*), while artists like Pheidias adorned many cities with their sculptures. At the same time the mobility of craftsmen in Classical Greece and their consequent originality and inventiveness must be a heritage from our Early Bronze Age when they were a logical consequence of the structure of Early Aegean societies and of the conditions under which the new professional population had emerged. The distinctively European – for such they are – traditions then established survived when the social structures that had evoked them changed. And changed they had even before the Homeric Age. The social organization of Classical Greece was notoriously different from that of the Late Bronze Age as described in Homer. The latter may have been just as different from that of the Early Bronze Age outlined here.

Indeed towards the close of the Early Aegean Age archaeologists can discern hints of changes tending in the directions realized by the Late Bronze Age. Stone battle-axes from Thrace and Macedonia, cord-ornamented vases from Central Greece, too, have been interpreted by many prehistorians as symbolizing the incursion of warrior bands from north of the Balkans. The hypothetical warriors might have constituted a ruling class and converted the communities they conquered into stratified societies of rulers and subjects. Be that as it may, some such stratification was certainly effected in North-west Anatolia, the Macedonian coastlands, and the whole of peninsular Greece in the Middle Helladic Age soon after 2000 B.C. In Greece the Early Helladic townships were violently destroyed and the Early Helladic culture replaced by another, termed 'Minyan'. This is sharply contrasted with the Early Helladic in ceramic traditions, burial practices and domestic architecture. And the same culture replaced the Early Troadic in Troy VI. In these circumstances the cultural changes used to distinguish Early from Middle Helladic must reflect an actual mass invasion and conquest. Unless the conquerors exterminated the defeated population – and sufficient Early Helladic traditions survive to make that unlikely – they presumably formed an aristocracy, ruling and exploiting tributary 'aboriginal' townsfolk and peasants.

The islands escaped the conquest. But in Crete at least a concentration of power and wealth had begun even before 2000 B.C. and led to a *de facto* division of society into ruling and subject classes. Local chieftains at Knossos and Mallia in Northern Central Crete and at Phaestos and Hagia Triadha in the South concentrated enough wealth and power to have built for them residences, so much more elaborate and sumptuous than any others as to deserve the name 'palaces'. They are in fact appropriate to kings, i.e. to chiefs so far raised above their fellow-tribesmen as to convert the latter into subjects.

The consequences will be examined in Chapter 9. Only one need be mentioned here. On the available evidence non-agricultural professionals preserved their traditional freedoms unimpaired. Now their freedom, we must repeat, was possible and actual just because the Urban Revolution had previously taken place in Egypt and Mesopotamia. The extractive industries and distributive systems that served Aegean craftsmen had been built up in reliance on Oriental capital. It was the effective and reliable markets of Egypt and Mesopotamia that alone made it worth while building and manning ships for overseas voyages, seeking out and opening up lodes of copper, silver, lead, and tin, and even growing crops for the market instead of just for subsistence.

(ii) THE COMMERCIAL EXPLORATION OF THE WESTERN MEDITERRANEAN

Tin was a commodity that Aegean peoples could always have disposed of profitably on those Oriental markets. They could not indeed produce it themselves, but they might have obtained it from Tuscany, Galicia, or even Cornwall. There is explicit evidence for Aegean maritime activity in the Central and Western Mediterranean quite soon after 2000 B.C. It may have begun before that date, but there are only the most ambiguous and questionable hints that it actually did. The earliest undoubted Aegean manufactures exported in that direction and identified up to date – a Middle Helladic vase from a Sicilian tomb and two Middle Cycladic vases reputedly found respectively in Marseilles harbour and on Minorca — are datable only between 1800 and 1500 B.C. The neatest pattern is obtained by supposing that the phenomena to be described below also began only after 2000 B.C., and expert opinion has recently veered almost unanimously in that direction and against a longer chronology formerly fashionable. Yet the arguments adduced are essentially negative and rather subjective. So we shall summarize the archaeological evidence here while insisting that its chronological place should on contemporary fashions be in a later chapter.

Supposed precursors of the Greek colonies of Classical times are represented mainly by cemeteries of collective tombs that appear rather abruptly in South-east Sicily, at Paestum a little south of Naples, in Sardinia, near Arles on the Rhône delta, and in Almeria (South-east Spain) and Southern Portugal. The fortified settlements to which the cemeteries belonged are known only at Los Millares, five miles up the Andorax from Almeria city, and at a couple of sites near the Tagus estuary. Collective burial seems an innovation in the West, but was practised from neolithic times on the East Mediterranean coasts. The coastal settlements, represented by the cemeteries, had been established very much where the Greek colonies in the West were actually planted in historical times; so the Paestum cemetery might belong to the prehistoric precursor of Cumae, the oldest Greek colony in the West, that near Arles to a forerunner of Marseilles, the first Greek foundation in South France.

But, I must insist, these cemeteries do not represent a single culture or even a single cycle in the sense that the cemeteries attached to the historical Greek colonies do, and none of the several cultures represented has an exact counterpart in the Aegean or anywhere in the East Mediterranean. Tomb types vary from place to place, and none have more than general analogies in the Aegean or the Levant. Grave goods vary similarly, and no assemblage as a whole can be precisely matched in Greece or Hither Asia. In particular not a single undoubted East Mediterranean manufacture (apart from one Middle Helladic vase not older than 1800 B.C.) has been found in an Italiote or West Mediterranean tomb, whereas hundreds of Greek vases imported from Athens, Corinth, or other workshops in Old Greece have been recovered from the cemeteries of Classical Syracuse, Cumae, or Emporion. In a word, if prospectors and merchants from the Aegean helped to found Bronze Age colonies on the coasts of Sicily, peninsular Italy, South France, South-east Spain, and Southern Portugal, they did not bring a complete material and ideological equipment with them, or maintain contacts with their homeland to keep them supplied with its manufactures as did the historical Greek colonists.

Yet throughout the area the populations included, albeit in varying proportions, representatives of a distinctive brachycranial racial type (plano-occipital steep-heads) that is known also in Cyprus and East Mediterranean lands, and as an intrusive element in Temperate Europe too (p. 144). Burial was everywhere collective, and the tombs were grouped in small cemeteries as in the East Mediterranean. The ossuaries, apart from natural caves, have a vaguely East Mediterranean air. The chambers are circular in plan in Sicily, South-east Spain, and Portugal, and nearly so in Italy, built above ground in corbelled masonry and buried in a cairn in Almeria and Algarve, but elsewhere rock cut, entered by a stepped pit in Italy and North-west Sicily (pit-caves), but by a passage in Portugal and South-east Sicily. In Sardinia each tomb consisted of several intercommunicating rock-cut chambers rectangular in plan, while the Arles tombs are long narrow galleries reached by a descending ramp.

Some accessories of funerary cult have a no less vaguely East Mediterranean look. The stone slabs that closed a South-east Sicilian tomb had been carved to suggest a female bust. A series of stelae from South France – only once found in association with a collective burial and that not at Arles – present a goddess in much the same stylization as the stele from Troy I. Limestone figurines from Sardinian tombs look like local copies of Cycladic idols. Highly conventionalized female figurines, painted on the phalange bones of horses, or engraved on limestone cylinders or slate plaques, are common in Almerian and Portuguese tombs. It looks as if in the West the old Fertility Goddess was becoming a Goddess of Death. After all, if all living

things spring from the womb of Mother Earth, it is to Her
bosom that they must return at death. It is this aspect of the
Mother Goddess that was especially emphasized in the
West. Now the Dead, the Ancestral Spirits who have thus
returned to Earth, may be regarded as potent intermediaries
between Her and their survivors and be invoked to inter-
cede for Her life-giving favour. Then a tomb would
become a shrine. South-east Sicilian rock-cut tombs and
some in Sardinia and built tombs in Almeria are in fact
preceded by ornate façades or forecourts that would form
an appropriate setting for the ceremonies of such a cult.

If the deceased were a spiritual chief, credited with
peculiar or exclusive influence with the numinous powers,
he could still and even better exercise his intercessory
function after his demise, as the Egyptian pharaohs reputedly did. The ancestral mausoleum would then become a
temple; the megalithic tombs to be considered in Chapter
8 could be thus interpreted. But there is no evidence for
Early Aegean practices tending in that direction. Still les:
Aegean was the erection of temples that were not tombs
This was done demonstrably only on Malta and Gozo.
The celebrated Maltese temples must be partly contemporary with the West Mediterranean cemeteries here considered and reproduce on a gigantic scale the ground plans
of local tombs. They had been enlarged and rebuilt several
times before they were deserted or put to a different use
not later than 1500 B.C. But they remain an isolated phenomenon in prehistoric Europe, to which only the Shetland
Islands have as yet offered a distant parallel.

In secular life most of the colonists whose tombs we
know were certainly farmers, as were most Early Aegean
townsmen. But, like the latter, they included a few professionals engaged in extractive, distributive, and secondary
industries. Copper was presumably mined in the Iberian

119

peninsula, Sardinia, and South France. Direct evidence for the smelting of copper ores comes from the Tagus region and from Los Millares in Almeria. At the latter site silver, too, was separated from copper and from lead. Two buttons of metallic tin from a sepulchral cave on the coast of Tuscany have been quoted as evidence that the small lodes of that province were already in exploitation. Being associated with a copper dagger of Early Minoan pattern, they do provide some slender justification for the thesis that Early Aegean communities were getting this vital metal from the West. The copper used in Sicily and South Italy must of course have been imported, but its distribution was so irregular or so expensive that it did not compete effectively with stone and bone. Indeed just at this period flint was being extracted and worked in regular factories round the Hyblaean range the products of which were exported over most of Sicily. At the same time the quarrying and exportation of obsidian from the Aeolian Islands were intensified.

Even in metalliferous regions copper was so inefficiently distributed or so extensively shipped overseas that splendidly flaked flint daggers and ground stone axes and adzes are much commoner than metal ones. So, though silver was extracted in Almeria, none has been found in contemporary tombs. To work the copper professional smiths were doubtless available, but their technique was relatively inferior. Metal vases were nowhere made. In Sicily and Italy daggers were cast in two-piece valve-moulds and attached to their hilts with rivets in imitation of Early Minoan models. But in the Iberian Peninsula and South France valve-moulds were unknown, and dagger-blades have notches instead of rivet holes for the hilt-attachment. The professional smiths are more likely to have been itinerants, serving many communities, than permanently resi-

dent in one village. No other full-time specialists need be
assumed. All pots were built up by hand without the use
of a wheel. None entail such exacting labour as the production of the huge jars and clay coffins built up by the
professional potters of Crete. Many vases from the Paestum
cemetery, some from Sicily and Sardinia, and a few from
Almeria do really look Aegean. But the ceramic assemblage
from even the Paestum cemetery cannot as a whole be
matched in any one Aegean or East Mediterranean assemblage.

Stone vases were made only in the Iberian Peninsula and
Malta. The former are of the simplest form and fashioned
in soft stone so that they demanded no professional skill and
afford no significant analogies with the East Mediterranean.
Some of the Maltese vases are real works of art and of
gigantic size. But full-time specialization can no more
be deduced from these than from the fine stone vessels of
pre-pottery neolithic Jarmo (p. 36), while the forms are
peculiar to the island. So too, though hard stones were
sometimes perforated to make beads, these are of simple
form and need not betray professional workmanship.
Seals and fine goldsmiths' work were unknown.

Some settlements certainly became secondary centres of
demand and obtained materials imported from overseas.
None of these was demonstrably of East Mediterranean
provenance. On the other hand beads of callaïs, jet, and
amber reached Los Millares in Almeria and Alcalá in
Portugal. They were reputedly fetched from Brittany,
England, and the Baltic respectively. If their sources have
been correctly determined, they should result from maritime trade along the Atlantic coasts, such as the Tartes-
sians were engaged in soon after 600 B.C.[78] And such trade
would surely have secured the yet more valuable tin from
Cornwall. Unfortunately the sources of callaïs and jet are

not so precisely defined and the – rather ambiguous – indications of connexions between Portugal and the British Isles point to the period 1800 to 1300 B.C. rather than to the third millennium. Even the temple-builders of Malta managed to secure obsidian and stones for querns and axes, but not apparently copper. The imports may have been brought as offerings by pious pilgrims or by involuntary visitors like St Paul and his company. But the islands became neither trading posts nor centres of a Bronze Age economy. They remained neolithic till occupied between 1600 and 1500 B.C. by parties of more warlike settlers who cremated their dead and interred their ashes among the ruins of the temples. Then Malta and Gozo became perhaps lairs for pirates rather than retreats for pilgrims or markets for merchants.

So the cemeteries just described in Italy, Sicily, and the West Mediterranean cannot be attributed to exact counterparts of the Greek and Phoenician colonies of the Iron Age in the same regions. If the corresponding settlements were founded, as the cemeteries' locations and some of their contents suggest, by voyagers from the East Mediterranean, these must have absorbed or been absorbed by contingents of the neolithic farmers who had been already established round their first landfalls. If the voyagers included prospectors and merchants, seeking raw materials for Aegean or Oriental markets, these allotted to satisfy local demands a far smaller fraction of their winnings than their compeers in the Aegean; all the silver they certainly did extract in Spain, all but two buttons of the tin they should have won in Tuscany, and any obtained by Atlantic trade from Cornwall must have been shipped 'home'. If they included professional smiths, the latter imparted hardly anything of their lore to native apprentices in Sardinia, South France, or Spain and Portugal; but of course prospectors, miners, and smelters are not necessarily masters of the arts of casting and forging. In any case the hypothetical mining and commercial ventures, supported by the Aegean market in the West Mediterranean, did not form the foundation for a genuine bronze industry there. In peninsular Italy the first effective machinery for the distribution of metal was to be based on the Central European system established between 1800 and 1600 B.C. Further west, save in Almeria, distribution was not effectively organized till the Late Bronze Age several centuries later and again on Central European rather than Aegean lines.

Nevertheless some actual colonization by East Mediterranean people does seem the best explanation for the phenomena cursorily surveyed in this section. On the analogy of the recorded Greek expansion westward, this colonization should have taken place by stages. According to recorded history Cumae, Syracuse, and other early colonies in Italy and Sicily were founded from Old Greece between 750 and 700 B.C., Massilia was founded from Italy about 600, her first daughter colonies on the Spanish coast a century later. So if, as the writer believes, the first East Mediterranean settlements or at least visits by Aegean traders and prospectors on the south-west coast of Italy cannot be later than 2000 B.C., Los Millares still need be no earlier than 1500! But in that case the account, to be given in Chapter 8, of a Megalithic religion as an ideological distortion of an Early Aegean quest for tin, amber, and gold will be untenable.

MISSIONARIES, TRADERS, AND WARRIORS IN TEMPERATE EUROPE

WHILE a distinctively European bronze industry was being established round the Aegean, a neolithic economy still persisted north of the Balkans, the Alps, and the Pyrenees. The Early Aegean Age corresponds in time to parts at least of Middle and Late Neolithic in Temperate Europe. But at least during the latter period ripples generated by the Urban Revolution were already disturbing the self-sufficiency of the peasant communities. At the same time 'political' events – migrations and conquests – were preparing the sociological foundations for a Bronze Age economy. Only a very superficial and highly simplified account of these momentous changes can be offered here.

(i) MISSIONARIES OF THE MEGALITHIC RELIGION

When we ask for evidence of those scarcely credible Atlantic voyages by prospectors and merchant venturers that should have brought Baltic amber and Cornish tin to the Aegean through Spain and Portugal or South France, we are referred, as in the Western Mediterranean, to collective tombs.[37] But so soon as we leave the coasts of South France, Spain, and Southern Portugal to survey the hinterland and the remoter Atlantic shores, the tombs can no longer be invoked as indices of colonization, but must be interpreted as monuments of a cult – 'the megalithic religion'. It is expressed for us in the erection of collective sepulchres, fulfilling the function and often reproducing the plans of the rock-cut chambers and corbelled vaults of the Mediterranean. But these tombs for the most part have been built of enormous stones above ground to be buried under cairns or barrows and are never grouped close together to form cemeteries. The magnitude of the stones employed in most of these structures justifies the application of the epithet 'megalithic' to them all. The monumental character of these isolated sepulchres and the stupendous labour expended on their erection at once prompts a question not raised by the cemeteries of collective tombs round the Mediterranean: were all members of the local community entitled to burial in these ossuaries, or only members of a noble lineage? Endorsement of the second alternative will be defended in the sequel.

Megalithic tombs of this kind but with wide local differences in plans, structural details, furniture, and burial rites are quite densely distributed in Portugal, Southern and Western France, Ireland, the western side of Britain and the north of Scotland, Northern Holland, North Germany, Denmark, and Sweden – in a word roughly along the Atlantic and North Sea coasts. Their diffusion has been attributed to descents from Northern Europe of forerunners of the Normans, or more often to a migrant race, commercial colonists or culture heroes from the East Mediterranean. In fact, however, megalithic tombs do not contain skeletons belonging only to a single racial type or relics that could characterize a single culture. In each main province the relics are those appropriate to one or more local cultures and are not found in association with collective burials only. Even when the same distinctive pottery is found in tombs of two provinces, as for instance in Brittany and round the Firth of Clyde in Scotland, tomb plans and other items of furniture diverge.

At the same time there is no evidence in most regions that the first building of megalithic tombs coincided with the beginnings of farming, still less of metallurgy. So in Brittany and Southern England and still more in North Germany and Denmark the earliest farming settlements are older than any collective tombs. In Brittany, the British Isles, and the whole of Northern Europe megalithic tombs are neolithic in the sense that the earliest burials in them are never accompanied by any metal gear or by articles shaped with metal tools. In these areas the first metal objects are associated with the Beaker-folk who arrived after the erection of the tombs, though they were sometimes admitted to burial therein (p. 145). It looks then as if the idea of building megalithic tombs was indeed diffused, but was adopted by various local societies without affecting other detectable aspects of their behaviour. But of course ideas can only be diffused by human agents, and these agents must settle down; the captain of a merchant vessel, for instance, by simply calling at a port could neither teach the natives to build megalithic tombs nor inspire them with the will to do so. It will help us to make a reasoned guess as to the character of its human vehicles, if we examine more closely the distribution of the idea's embodiments in Britain.

The megalithic tombs of Britain[79] may be called exotic in that all are variants on types evenly distributed throughout Western and Northern Europe but nevertheless contain remains of an insular native culture. Three principal groups may be distinguished on the basis of tomb plans: the Cotswold-Severn group on both sides of the Severn estuary and extending eastward onto the downs of Wiltshire and Berkshire; the Clyde-Carlingford group in South-west Scotland, Northern Ireland, and in the Isle of Man; and the Pentland group on the Orkneys and the adjacent parts of mainland Scotland. All tombs in the first two groups, and a substantial minority in the third, were covered by extravagantly long cairns, out of all proportion to the little

burial chamber at one end, recalling the mounds raised over
some members of earlier neolithic societies in England and
east of the North Sea. Cotswold-Severn tombs were first
built after the downs and probably South Wales, too, had
already been colonized by Windmill Hill peasants as
described in Chapter 5 and contain a typically Windmill
Hill furniture. Tombs of the remaining groups do constitute the earliest evidence for neolithic settlement in their
respective provinces, but contain an equally British furniture.

The unique record from the Orcadian island of Rousay[80]
allows us to formulate concretely the question who were
entitled to burial in a megalithic tomb, posed on p. 125.
The fifteen cairns covering megalithic chambers, surviving
on this small mountainous island, occur in groups, each
corresponding to a natural unit of settlement, still defined
by a cluster of crofts and a church or church site. Three
cairns overlook the Frotoft valley where there are now
twenty-one crofts; two cairns overlook eight farms,
collectively known as Brinyon; five stand in and around
the Sourin valley still farmed by fifty crofting households.
So our question can be restated thus: Did only three
neolithic households farm the land now worked by twenty-
one in Frotoft and did five alone represent the neolithic
precursors of the fifty crofts in Sourin? Or was each of the
units just defined already settled by a group of households
as today, of which one alone in each unit area was so
exalted above the rest as to boast a megalithic family vault?
There is no reason why a neolithic economy should not
have supported a population comparable in density to that
maintained by subsistence farming and fishing in the eigh-
teenth century when there were 400 communicants, i.e.
adults, on the island; in the New Stone Age the island
boasted appreciable herds of deer in addition to the game

that still survives. The number of interments in the megalithic chambers of Rousay – twenty-five in Midhowe, only
three in Ramsay which is larger – is relatively small – as
indeed throughout the British Isles. Could such a household have erected so monumental a family vault? The
second alternative is surely the more plausible. Each tomb
should have belonged to a noble or leader and his (or her)
family. The labour force required for building his tomb
would be supplied by his followers.

But considering their distribution, not only on Rousay
but throughout the British Isles, a megalithic tomb should
be compared to a church rather than a castle, their noble
occupants to Celtic saints rather than to Norman barons.
Those saints did travel about and settle in the regions where
megalithic tombs still stand. They did gather about them
lay disciples from a devout peasantry. Their aim, as Adam-
nan[81] says of those who had gone from Ireland to Orkney,
was doubtless 'to find a solitude'. But they did not plan to
fast to death there or yet to feed themselves unaided.

Wherever a holy man set up as a hermit in a cave or
shack, numbers of local peasants gathered round him eager
to renounce their land and calling and enter a community
of devout farmers.[82] Collective tombs would, we saw on
p. 119, be also shrines if their occupants were credited with
peculiar spiritual powers. Are not the megalithic tombs of
Britain the counterparts of the little chapels founded by
Welsh and Irish saints in much the same parts of the British
Isles? If so, their founders might be called megalithic saints
and owe their authority and status to spiritual prestige
rather than temporal power.

The hypothesis of missionaries from the south-west win-
ning the allegiance of a British neolithic peasantry by their
reputation for sanctity or magic power would neatly
explain the transfer to Orkney or the Clyde coasts of a

peculiarly British material culture combined with an exotic
funerary architecture. Like Celtic missionaries the megalithic saints would have sailed to the coasts of Scotland,
Ireland, and the remoter isles inspired by equally unworldly
motives but accompanied by neolithic English or Armorican peasants, eager no doubt to join a community of pious
farmers, but also to go on farming and rear families. For
that their saintly leaders chose locations best adapted to the
primitive rural economy and rude equipment of their pious
disciples; megalithic tombs are in fact conspicuously
situated on just the sort of soil best suited for neolithic
farming.

It may be instructive to pursue the analogy further.
The Celtic saints were inspired by a faith that had originated
in the Eastern Mediterranean as our megalithic religion
supposedly did. But the special version of that faith to
which Celtic saints gave expression, while owing much to
Egyptian hermits, is believed to have assumed its distinctive
form in the Western Mediterranean or more precisely in
South France. And it is with South France, rather than
Portugal, that the architecture of British megalithic tombs
has most in common. On the other hand our Celtic saints
were members of one Church, an organized society
equipped not only with a formidable body of dogma, fixed
and perpetuated by a written tradition, but also with an
equally established ritual, likewise prescribed by written
texts. But no such organization at all can be imagined in
the centuries round about 2000 B.C. The missionaries had
no sacred books to define and preserve their faith; for they
were as illiterate as everyone else outside the valleys of the
Nile, the Tigris-Euphrates, and the Indus. Communications
in a densely wooded continent, 2,000 years before the
Romans had built the first network of roads, or by sea in
vessels fashioned with stone tools, were incomparably more

precarious and less frequent than even in the Dark Ages. If even then the Christian Church could be rent by heresies and schisms, how much more might numerous and bigoted sects be expected in the megalithic religion. A superficial reflection of such sectarian differences can be detected in local divergences of sepulchral architecture – divergences that cannot be enumerated in a book like this and have not been at all exhaustively catalogued in even the most technical manuals.

Of course sectarian differences may have gone deeper than funerary ritual or even eschatological beliefs. There are archaeological grounds for suspecting that they affected also social structures and the material means of propagating the faith. Megalithic societies in Britain have been presented as peaceful farmers, bound by religious devotion alone to unworldly holy men. But even the later servants of a God of Love could become prince-bishops enriched by the exploitation of a semi-servile peasantry or warrior prelates. The Mother Goddess, whom the megalithic missionaries may have worshipped as a Goddess of Death, could more easily become a Goddess of War. She does in fact at times assume martial attributes; in some Spanish and Portuguese tombs her abbreviated image is associated with a dagger; the sculptured stelae of South France, mentioned on p.118, represent a female figure who carries an axe, surely a battle-axe. The same figure, more summarily depicted save that the martial function of her axe is explicitly indicated, is found carved or painted on the walls of a few chamber tombs, cut in the chalk of Champagne (Dept. Marne).

Now these chalk-cut chambers are the most Mediter-ranean-looking tombs in the Temperate Zone of Europe. They may therefore be regarded as the sepulchres of the first missionaries of the megalithic faith to reach North-east France. But here the missionaries appear also as secular chieftains, the war-leaders of a militant population. In Champagne the sculptured tombs just described are juxtaposed to simpler tombs that must be the resting-places of their followers. The former are spacious and divided into chamber and antechamber; they contain not more than eight skeletons; but the grave goods comprise a few imported luxuries – beads of amber, callaïs, and gold, and small objects of copper. The remaining tombs are much smaller in size, but normally contain forty or more skeletons, while the furniture is poorer and includes no valuable imports. The furniture of tombs of both classes represents the material culture, the equipment, of one society of warrior hunters, stock-breeders, and cultivators. No item in their equipment is of specifically Mediterranean origin. The domestic stock and cereals might have been introduced by Danubian peasants who had certainly reached the Marne (p. 61). The actual instruments of production and weapons – flint axes and their antler mounts, transverse arrow-heads – can all be derived from mesolithic types used by hunter-fishers who may have been in occupation of the region since Atlantic times.

Thus we should have in Champagne a stratified society formed by the imposition of megalithic chiefs on a superstitious but warlike native peasantry. The chiefs would have introduced the chamber tomb and the Goddess carved upon its walls. They might also have introduced a curious ritual perversion of neolithic surgery that was practised also in South France where their Goddess was represented on stelae; so many skulls from Marne tombs have been trephined as far to exceed the numbers that would choose to submit to this painful and perilous operation for rational curative ends. But their followers on adopting the faith would also have gained admission to the privilege of burial in collective tombs, albeit inferior to those of their leaders. In the sequel it would seem these chiefs' descendants led bands of followers not to found devout communities in solitudes but to seize lands already occupied by neolithic farmers.

In the course of this conquering expansion both sepulchral architecture and social structure suffered modification. So near as the Paris basin where the Marne joins the Seine and the Oise, the chambers, so easily cut in the chalk of Champagne, were replaced by truly megalithic tombs of a peculiar type – a long narrow gallery entered from a shallow antechamber through a porthole slab – that is termed a Paris cist. Their furniture is identical with that of the Marne chambers and an absurdly high proportion of their occupants had been trephined. So the culture common to both groups is designated Seine-Oise-Marne, abbreviated SOM.[83] But there is no distinction between chieftains' and commoners' tombs; all alike reposed in Paris cists. In the emigration the leaders had been assimilated to their followers as far as burial status was concerned.

Typical Paris cists, appropriately furnished with SOM types, illustrate an expansion of the culture, westward to Normandy, Jersey, and Brittany, north-east through Belgium to Westphalia and Hesse, and eventually to South Sweden and Denmark, and southwards at least to the Cevennes, if not to the Mediterranean coasts. Finally, an expansion through the Belfort Gap to the Upper Rhine and Aar is documented by a few ruined tombs and by the Horgen culture that succeeds Cortaillod and Michelsberg in settlements on the Lakes of Zürich and Neuchâtel; for Horgen is essentially the SOM culture of France.

These phenomena must be explained in terms of an actual emigration of devout but land-hungry bands of herdsmen from the SOM tribes who established themselves and built their tombs on fresh pastures. But the territories thus annexed had all been previously colonized by one or more layers of neolithic farmers. South Sweden and Denmark had even been overrun by tribes of warrior herdsmen who had imposed their Battle-axe cultures on still earlier farmers (p. 135). In Brittany and Jersey megalithic saints were already established among Western peasants, while in South France groups of farmers and herdsmen had already adopted one version or another of the megalithic faith. The archaeological record leaves it uncertain whether the SOM crusaders had exterminated the earlier populations, ruled them as a spiritual and military aristocracy, or simply fused with them. Perhaps the last alternative is the most likely; round the Baltic in any case so much of the older native equipment reappears in Paris cists that their furniture illustrates a genuine mixed culture, but in this case the herding economy, associated with the SOM culture, had already become general or been introduced by the herdsmen who brought the Battle-axe cultures.

Whether in its pacific or its militant aspect the megalithic religion did nothing to foster those kinds of tradition that are here regarded as most distinctively European. In Portugal and France where it was accepted most generally and maintained most stubbornly no local bronze industry was developed much before 1000 B.C. In Britain it was only after the spiritual aristocracy of megalithic saints had been replaced by a military aristocracy of Beaker-folk that metal-workers and traders began to find a local market for their wares and to create an original and vigorous insular bronze industry about 1800 B.C. In North Germany, Denmark, and Sweden it was among Battle-axe herdsmen rather than among any group of megalith-builders that craftsmen were eventually to find patrons after 1500. That is not to say that megalithicism made no enduring contributions to European traditions. On the contrary, I suspect that behind many of the popular superstitions of Portugal, Brittany, and Ireland, and even in local peculiarities of Christianity, there lurk survivals of a megalithic tradition. But this is not the place, nor am I the man, to undertake an evaluation of their importance in the moulding of modern Europe. Technical and scientific traditions are less controversial and their appreciation less subjective.

(ii) WARRIOR HERDSMEN IN TEMPERATE EUROPE

The S O M tribes are only one of several groups of warlike pastoralists who emerged all over Temperate Europe from the Caspian to the North Sea in the Late Neolithic phase. Now, as Krichevskiĭ,[84] a brilliant Russian prehistorian who died prematurely in the siege of Leningrad, pointed out, an economy that emphasized stock-breeding and hunting would really be the most productive method of exploiting the soil of Europe with a neolithic equipment. At the same time stock-breeding, concentrating economic power in the hands of males, is normally associated with a patriarchal order of society. Cattle, as an easily movable form of wealth, offer a substantial reward to raiders and so a material inducement to more serious and frequent fighting. This form of wealth is more usually privately owned than is land and it can multiply. Finally, opportunities for accumulating wealth in herds and their differential multiplication, together with the need for leaders in serious warfare, foster economic differentiation within society and the elevation of chieftains invested with economic power. Krichevskiĭ, therefore, suggested that the emergence of warlike herding tribes in Late Neolithic Europe was just the result of the internal economic development of older neolithic societies and the separation from the latter of the

134

groups that had been the first to concentrate upon the more profitable pursuit of stock-breeding.

In fact such tribes of warlike herdsmen do first become archaeologically recognizable on the fringe of the fertile tracts of löss and loam primarily occupied by neolithic farmers or on sandy tracts and heaths between these fertile regions. For instance, in Jutland the Battle-axe herdsmen first appeared on the inland heaths while megalithic farmers tilled the richer soils along the coasts. Between the Elbe and the Weser and again on the Hondsrug in Holland the earliest Battle-axe barrows seem just to avoid the area thickly sprinkled with the megalithic tombs of more agricultural farmers. Similar distributions can be observed in Thuringia and beyond the Vistula down to the edge of the parklands, thickly settled by Tripolye farmers. On the other hand it has been contended that some or all of these pastoralists were fresh immigrants who had invaded Central and North-western Europe from the Pontic steppes or even from Central Asia. Let us postpone a decision between Krichevskii's thesis and that of fresh immigrations and examine the herding societies as represented in the archaeological record. In addition to the SOM culture, already described, and some more localized megalith-builders in South France, the herdsmen are represented by two or three major cycles of cultures: the Ochre Grave cultures of South Russia, the Battle-axe cultures of Central and Northern Europe, and the Globular Amphora-makers of Central Europe and Podolia.[85] All are known exclusively from graves; no regular settlements have been identified. That might suggest nomadism. But the herding of cattle in woodlands does not involve that sort of nomadism familiar among the shepherd tribes of the dry steppes of Hither Asia and vividly described in the Old Testament. More apt comparisons can be made with Nilotic and East

135

African tribes like the Azandi of the Sudan or the Banya-kole of Tanganyika. Indeed the only neolithic herding societies whose habitations are known owing to unique environmental circumstances lived in clusters of commodious stone houses, continuously inhabited and rebuilt three or more times on the same site at Rinyo and Skara Brae in Orkney.[86]

(a) The Pontic Ochre Grave Culture

On the grassy steppes that extend from the Caucasian foothills and the Lower Volga round the Black Sea to the Dobrudja and on the adjacent parkland to the north the earliest food-producing societies yet known are represented by clusters of barrows covering shaft-graves (Russian *yamy*) containing skeletons liberally sprinkled with red ochre. The culture thus illustrated is termed the Ochre Grave culture;[37] its development has been traced by Russian archaeologists through three main phases – Early, Middle, and Late Pontic or Kuban (Kuban properly refers to a special version of the Ochre Grave culture on the northern slopes of the Caucasus where the Early phase can be subdivided into I and II).

The barrow clusters[87] should correspond to groups of families who grazed their stock and cultivated millet or one and the same stretch of steppe. The Early Pontic pastoralists' equipment was still purely neolithic save in the Kuban basin. Even there the only metal tools, weapons, and ornaments had all been imported from beyond the range and were available only to a few great chiefs. Chiefs were indeed recognized also on the more northern steppes. One had been interred near Dniepropetrovsk with a two-wheeled cart or covered wagon in accordance with the ritual established for the first Sumerian kings. The graves of two others were covered with rudely anthropomorphic

stelae. The barrow covering the burial of a third was supported by a ring of stone slabs, carved with geometric
patterns. But in the Kuban basin twenty-four enormous
barrows look like the tombs of veritable kings. That at
Maikop (Early Kuban I), for instance, covered a wooden
chamber containing the remains of two attendants besides
the chief. And he was provided with a canopy, spangled
with figures of bulls and lions in gold and silver, ornaments
of precious metal and gems, vases of stone, gold and silver,
and weapons of unalloyed copper. The latter are of types
known to have been manufactured in Transcaspia and
North-eastern Iran,[88] and all the rest are imports from some
centre of higher civilization in Transcaucasia.

Somehow or other tribes grazing their flocks and herds
along the rivers that flow northward from the metalliferous Caucasus had secured a share in the wealth of richer,
partially urbanized societies living south of the range.
Perhaps they were already driving their stock up to summer
pastures in the high mountains and from transhumance
went on to raiding. Perhaps prospectors and miners, trained
in the applied science of Mesopotamia and relying on its
markets for their livelihood, were ready working the ores
of Ciscaucasia and had to conciliate the local population
with valuable presents. In either case tribal chiefs would
secure the major share of the booty or the gifts and by this
very fact were made economically independent of their
followers and so could raise themselves above society,
aping the divine kings of Oriental civilization. None of the
wealth thus acquired was used in Early Kuban times for
the development of a local bronze industry. But some of the
techniques and inventions of Mesopotamian crafts – particularly the wheel, significantly associated with royal
funerals – were adopted and applied locally and transmitted
to kindred tribes on the steppes further to the north-west.

In the succeeding Middle Kuban-Pontic period the erection of royal tombs and the importation of Oriental manufactures alike ceased. But though wealth was less concentrated, the total surplus was now large enough to support a local metal industry. Descendants or apprentices of the hypothetical metal-workers who, relying on the Mesopotamian demand, had discovered the Caucasian ores and exploited them for the Mesopotamian market, now began producing for local consumption. The local demand was in fact effective enough to encourage the discovery and opening-up of the richer deposits round the Urals where an outpost of Caucasian metallurgy was soon established. Smiths produced tools and weapons, modelled on Meso-potamian types but adapted to local fashions, and highly original ornaments, some cast by the lost wax process. No smithies or smiths' graves have been identified – both are known in Late Kuban times – so metal was probably distributed and worked by itinerant merchant-artificers as in the Bronze Age of Central Europe. As there, they some-times had to bury their stock-in-trade as hoards, a couple of which have been recovered. But even on the northern steppes the distribution of metal was efficient enough to allow copper tools to be used even for rough work like excavating chamber tombs.

By this time some trade with the Aegean may have made up for the loss of Transcaspian and Transcaucasian markets. In a limited part of the old Ochre Grave province – along the Black Sea coasts from Odessa eastward, a little way up the Dniepr, the Donetz, the Don, and the Manych and thence across the isthmus into Daghestan – the older shaft graves (*yamy*) were replaced by a new tomb type, called by the Russians a *catacomb*. But a *catacomb* is just a chamber-tomb entered through a stepped pit, i.e. a pit-cave, such as had been fashionable on the Cyclades and Euboea in Early

Aegean times, but was used also in Hither Asia as far east as Assyria.[89] At the same time appeared among the long-headed steppe folk the first round-heads, just as had happened throughout the Mediterranean at the dawn of the Bronze Age there. But round the Black Sea some of these artificially elongated their heads by annular cranial deformation – a distortion that had been practised in Cyprus and North Syria even before 3000 B.C.[90] It really looks as if Aegean or East Mediterranean ideas and persons of East Mediterranean racial stock were filtering up the rivers from the Black Sea coasts. Are there perhaps, awaiting discovery, Aegean trading posts where the Greeks planted their colonies a thousand years later? But the only concrete result of such commerce yet discovered by archaeologists is a couple of faience beads.

At the same time the use of cord-impressions to decorate Middle Pontic pots and finds of stone battle-axes in Middle Kuban graves disclose ambiguous relations with the warrior herdsmen of the woodlands to the north and north-west. Less ambiguous testimony is afforded by the distribution of hammer pins – a distinctively Pontic-Caucasian ornament, fashionable at the very beginning of the Middle Kuban period. Versions of such pins, locally made in each case, occur on the one hand in royal tombs at Alaca in Central Anatolia, in Troy II and in Middle Helladic Lerna in Greece, and on the other in Battle-axe graves near Moscow, in Sammland east of the Baltic, and in Central Germany as well as in a megalithic tomb in Denmark. This distribution shows that the Pontic herdsmen could at least act as intermediaries in the transmission of ideas from the civilized East to a still barbarian West. They must for instance have been the agents through whom the idea of a wheel, rules for its manufacture, and even the superstition that wheeled vehicles must be buried in royal tombs were passed on from Mesopotamian city-states to Late Neolithic tribal societies in Temperate Europe.

The Pontic steppe folk were only an eastern wing of a loose continuum of mobile herding societies among whom fruitful intercourse can be demonstrated though its drift may be debated. It could, for instance, be contended[91] that the kings buried at Alaca Höyük and in the Shaft Graves of Mycenae were sprung from our steppe folk and were responsible for introducing Indo-European languages, Hittite and Greek respectively, into Anatolia and Greece and that the various Battle-axe peoples to the north and north-west who might have been ancestors of the Celts, the Teutons, and the Slavs were offshoots from Ochre Grave societies. But in the present state of archaeology in South Russia and the Ukraine, these relations could perfectly well be reversed!

(b) Battle-axe Peoples

The epithet 'Battle-axe' is applied to a number of distinct cultures and peoples – 'Single-grave' in Jutland, North Germany, and Holland; 'Boat-axe' in Sweden and east of the Baltic; 'Rzuczewo' in Sammland; 'Fatyanovo' in Central Russia; Middle Dniepr; Galician; Oder; 'Saxo-Thuringian' in Bohemia, Central and South-west Germany; and several others.[37] All exhibit to archaeologists certain abstract behaviour patterns in common, notably those of depositing battle-axes with drooping blades in males' graves and of ornamenting pots with cord impressions; toy battle-axes of clay were actually buried with Fatyanovo and Boat-axe boys! But the shapes of the battle-axes and the pots vary from group to group. Like Ochre Grave folk, these several peoples are known almost exclusively from small cemeteries of barrows – Single Grave, Saxo-Thuringian, Middle Dniepr – or flat graves – Boat-axe, Fatyanovo, Oder. Once more the cemeteries and the barrows within them were used for burials over several generations. During this time fashions changed so that chronological phases in the development of each culture can be detected. Radio-carbon dates of 2500 and 2250 B.C. respectively have been assigned to two Dutch burials, the relative age of which is unfortunately indeterminate.

All combined some cereal cultivation with hunting and stock-breeding. All can be regarded as patriarchally organized in view of occasional satî burials. Chiefs can be recognized only in Central Russia, Western Germany, and Switzerland. Save perhaps in the Ukraine, none of these groups used metal regularly; indeed their eponymous weapons are copies of, and substitutes for, copper axes. Only the Fatyanovo people on the Volga are known to have possessed wheeled vehicles; the clay wheels of a toy cart were buried with a Fatyanovo child. Horses' bones occur in some Fatyanovo, Galician, and Ukrainian graves, but might have belonged to game animals.

In the earlier phases of each culture its authors seem studiously to have avoided territories occupied by Tripolye, Danubian, TRB, or other farmers; thus early Battle-axe barrows and stray battle-axes of early type are conspicuously absent from those areas in Jutland, between the Elbe and the Weser, and on the Hondsrug in Holland, where megalithic tombs are concentrated. Later they encroached on territories formerly occupied by peasants. In Northern Europe indeed late battle-axes or battle-axe pots are found in some collective tombs, but only with the latest interments therein. Perhaps Battle-axe warriors had married into the old megalithic families, thus earning the right to burial in the family vault. But they built no new megalithic tombs. For they did not adopt the megalithic ideology and replaced the former spiritual leaders by military ones. Similarly in Switzerland the replacement of the SOM-Horgen settlements by others yielding cord-ornamented pots and other types appropriate to the Saxo-Thuringian Battle-axe culture should symbolize the formation of a composite society dominated by Battle-axe traditions. In such more or less mixed cultures it may be suspected that the Battle-axe component formed a sort of aristocracy. Where, as apparently in Denmark, the intrusive culture replaced the old, extermination or complete enslavement cannot be ruled out.

Only the Usatova culture on the western shore of the Black Sea reveals more of the structure of a stratified society, but in this case the 'upper class' might as plausibly be termed 'Ochre Grave' as 'Battle-axe'. At Usatova near Odessa we are lucky enough to know the habitations of the living as well as the graves of the dead and among the latter two contrasted cemeteries. In the rural economy cultivation carries on the old Tripolye tradition, but stock-breeding has assumed enormously enhanced importance. And among the stock swine sink to a negligible proportion (2 per cent) while goats or sheep and horses increase proportionately to 48 and 13 per cent respectively; kine account for most of the balance. Industrially pottery fired and painted in the Tripolye technique is balanced by dark-faced cord-ornamented vases. Clay figurines mark a survival of the peasants' fertility cult of a Mother Goddess, but she has been so conventionalized that not even her sex is recognizable. The cultivators were interred in simple pit-graves, sometimes, however, accompanied by metal weapons and ornaments. Their pastoral overlords were buried under barrows supported by a ring of upright slabs at least one of which had been carved like a stele. Under each barrow, in addition to the central grave containing the principal interment, eccentric pits in the subsoil contained remains of slaves or attendants or ritual deposits – animal bones, a figurine or a conventional carving of a bull's head. While a few amber beads or silver rings accompanied nobles, nobles and commoners alike could afford copper daggers and axes.

Usatova and some less well-known kindred communities could thus produce and concentrate enough to constitute a market for metals and to support professional smiths, resident or perambulating. Metals, as well as amber, they might have secured as an incident in a quite hypothetical long-distance traffic with Troy or the Aegean along routes, marked by no recognized archaeological finds, leading from Transylvanian or Slovakian lodes of ore and the amber coast of Sammland to unidentified trading posts on the Black Sea. If their smiths had been trained by the prospectors, postulated as working those lodes on p. 61, or in the Aegean, they had mastered no refinements of technique. Like their fellow-workers in Almeria and South France (p.120), they knew nothing of casting in valve-moulds but clumsily imitated Aegean types by the primitive open-hearth process. The local West Pontic school of metallurgy never advanced from this low level, and after 1500 B.C. was replaced by exponents of the Central European tradition and Hungarian products. Had the local smiths been reduced to the lower class in the incipient class-division of Usatova society and thus deprived of initiative? Or was it that all trade with the Aegean had been diverted to the new Brenner route?

In so far as Battle-axe warriors constituted aristocracies, they should have helped to concentrate a social surplus and so to make effective a demand for metal. We shall in fact find that Early Bronze Age chieftains in Poland and Central Germany and Middle Bronze Age ranchers in Denmark and over large areas in Central Europe who were the best patrons of local smiths, can be regarded as descended from local Battle-axe groups, but the affiliation in each case is rather problematical and indirect. No doubt Battle-axe herdsmen were protagonists of a patriarchal organization. But once more Baden, TRB, and probably even SOM communities were equally patriarchal. Contacts, hostile or pacific, were certainly multiplied by the relative mobility of herding tribes and the diffusion of ideas was thus accelerated. The distribution of Pontic hammer pins to Denmark, Central Germany, and Sammland concretely illustrates this result. But it was only after Battle-axe warrior herdsmen had joined forces with Beaker warrior traders that they became effective agents in the diffusion of progressive ideas.

(iii) BEAKER TRADERS

The last warrior group to appear in the archaeological record from Western and Central Europe played a far more constructive part than those hitherto mentioned. For though they travelled fast and far in small well-armed bands, their objectives were not only pastures and arable lands, but also raw materials for trade and industry, and smiths accompanied them. They again are known almost exclusively from graves and are most easily identified by a clay drinking cup of distinctive technique, form, and decoration, traditionally termed a 'bell beaker' or just a 'beaker'. They are therefore familiarly known as Beaker-folk. But their archaeological individuality[37] is not expressed solely in the peculiarities of their funerary and domestic pottery. They everywhere included persons of an equally distinctive round-headed physical type (plano-occipital steep-heads is the technical expression) so that it may be legitimate to speak of a Beaker race. Everywhere

their graves are furnished with equally distinctive armaments – bowmen's equipment and flat-tanged knife-
daggers.

Their bodies and characteristic pots and arms are found
in flat graves, sometimes grouped in little cemeteries, in
Upper Italy, along the Danube from Budapest through
Austria to Bavaria, then through Moravia and Bohemia
to the Upper Vistula and Oder and thence all across
Central and Western Germany just into Belgium and Holland. They are just as widely distributed in Western
Europe, but there were normally buried in collective
tombs, though in no case were they the builders of these.
Beakers are very common in the chamber-tombs round the
Tagus estuary and in the later megalithic tombs of Portugal
and Western Spain. They are fairly widespread in the rest
of Spain, occurring in three or four corbelled tholos tombs
at Los Millares and in several other Almerian cemeteries.
Plenty have been found in rock-cut tombs in Sardinia, and
there are even a few from Sicily and from a cave on the
African side of the Straits of Gibraltar. Beakers are very
common in all kinds of collective tombs and sepulchral
caves round the Pyrenees and in South France. There is
another big cluster in Brittany and the Channel Islands,
both in the earlier megalithic (passage) graves and in the
intrusive Paris cists, but only two have been recovered
from tombs of the latter kind in the Paris basin itself.

Some of the beakers in each and all of these widely
separated centres preserve a standard pattern – that of the
pan-European beaker – so faithfully that no long interval
of time can separate the arrival of Beaker-folk in each
centre. But sometimes at least they settled down, mingling
somehow with the local populations and adopting some of
their behaviour patterns. The most obvious archaeological
consequence is firstly the formation of local styles of

beakers and then an assimilation of beakers to local ceramic fashions that symbolizes the formation of mixed cultures. A band of Beaker-folk, bringing with them a local Rhenish style, invaded the British Isles and initiated a Bronze Age there. But these, labelled B1, were followed by other bands (labelled B2, C and A) with mixed cultures as will appear below.

Everywhere Beaker-folk used copper, albeit sparingly, so that they must have been served by some rather inefficient machinery for its distribution. Ornaments of gold, amber, and callaïs also are found in their graves, while the major concentrations of beakers are significantly located on natural trade routes. Beaker-folk therefore at least comprised traders, and their journeyings were to some extent trading expeditions. There are good grounds for thinking that Beaker-folk crossed the Alps by the Brenner Pass and thus opened up what was to be the most vital channel for trade between Central Europe and the Mediterranean world. Smiths, masters of the technique of casting, but probably not in valve-moulds, doubtless travelled with the bands; the association of a stone mould with a beaker in a Moravian grave marks this as the oldest burial of a craftsman known in Europe. It is not so clear whether any Beaker-folk possessed the geological and chemical knowledge needed for starting up mining and smelting operations. It is quite certain that they could not themselves produce the surplus needed for establishing a metallurgical industry and could find neither in the Western Mediterranean nor among the barbarian tribes of Temperate Europe a reliable and effective market that should justify the creation of machinery for the regular extraction and distribution of metal.

Most authorities believe that the Beaker-folk as we know them originated in the Iberian peninsula, most probably round the Tagus estuary in Portugal. On the other hand there are some plausible arguments in favour of a Beaker cradle in Central Europe – in Czechoslovakia or Western Germany – while an African origin has also been suggested. The metallurgical techniques that Beaker-folk diffused were of course East Mediterranean – their daggers were mounted in a manner that had been distinctive of Egypt since Predynastic times[92] – though their products are inferior in every respect to Early Aegean and Oriental types. The most striking physical type represented among Beaker-folk is likewise believed to be East Mediterranean; it is represented also in the early cemetery near Paestum in Italy, mentioned on p. 116. We might then imagine that this race had been a constituent of the maritime colonization postulated in the last chapter, and that in Portugal this commercial element separated out from the rest of the colonizing peasants to form a sort of gypsy society.

In any case, it must be assumed, Beaker-folk replaced the spiritual aristocracy of megalith-builders; for they secured admission to the privilege of burial in megalithic tombs. In South France and round the Pyrenees the new ruling class was completely absorbed; the old ideology continued to find expression in the erection of megalithic tombs and there was no further expansion of metallurgy or trade. In the rest of the Peninsula the Beaker-folk – or at least their beakers – died out, but so did the practice of collective burial, and new groups emerged. In Brittany too, Beaker-folk replaced the older aristocracies, but adopted their ideology and failed to transform their economy into one of Bronze Age type.[93] The few Beaker-folk who had reached the Paris basin were simply engulfed in S O M societies and left no trace of their presence beyond two beakers. In Central Europe composite societies emerged in which the rank of the Beaker-folk is uncertain. Along the Danube and on the Upper Elbe Beaker traditions were blended with those of Baden, Bodrogkeresztur and T R B communities and sometimes of Battle-axe peoples too. In Central and Western Germany Beaker-folk were fused with different Battle-axe groups; they borrowed the latter's battle-axes and their practice of burial under barrows and indeed preserved little more than the patterns on their beakers. Even the latter in technique are more like Battle-axe pots, decorated in the Beaker style; they might have been made by Battle-axe wives for Beaker husbands!

Bands from such composite societies crossed the North Sea (as B2 and C Beaker-folk) to spread from the east coasts of Britain across the island and eventually, from the Severn and Clyde estuaries, into Ireland. These newcomers together with the earlier, B1, invaders replaced the aristocracy of megalithic saints and suppressed their religion. Sometimes indeed a Beaker chief did consecrate his victory by marrying into the old ruling house and so was eventually interred in the family tomb. But no more megalithic tombs were built, and individual interment, generally under round barrows, replaced collective burial. As places of cult instead of funerary monuments, sacred enclosures, encircled by a ring of huge upright stones or by a bank and ditch, were laid out. But these incorporate older native conceptions, being just versions of the 'henge monuments' described on p. 66. For the various intrusive Beaker groups can have formed but a very thin ruling class and were eventually absorbed in the older neolithic population. Ere then they had revolutionized the islands' economy. Not only had they promoted stock-breeding as against cultivation and the growing of the hardier cereal, barley, in preference to wheat. They did at least foster the exploitation of Cornish tin, of the copper ores of Ireland and Highland Britain, and of Irish gold. And they maintained some sort of commercial relations with their Continental starting points.

Thus a Bronze Age in Britain really began under the auspices of Beaker-folk, but always in reliance on the East Mediterranean surplus. For by the time C Beaker-folk set out for Britain, the East Mediterranean market had been brought within the reach of Central European producers by the discovery of the Brenner route. But prospectors, miners, smelters, and smiths may already have reached Great Britain and Ireland by Atlantic seaways in the boats of megalithic saints.

CHAPTER 9

THE FOUNDATION OF A EUROPEAN CIVILIZATION

ORIENTAL or Early Aegean prospectors had very probably discovered the metal resources of Central and Western Europe before 2000 B.C. There competition for easily cultivable land since the close of the Middle Neolithic and the displacements of pastoral tribes in the Late Neolithic by aggravating fighting must have led to an appreciation of the deficiencies of stone weapons and induced a desire for more efficient metal substitutes. Some concentration of wealth in the hands of local war-chiefs and the more prosperous ranchers would create a potentially effective market for metal gear so soon as supplies were made available, but would scarcely suffice to induce the requisite labour force to engage on the hazards of extraction and distribution. An adequate inducement was supplied by an Aegean market, close at hand, when the Minoans of Crete and subsequently the Mycenaeans of Mainland Greece had accumulated and concentrated sufficient wealth to build an urban civilization of their own. This they accomplished only with the aid of fresh drafts on the Oriental surplus made available by an intensified concentration of wealth in Egypt and Mesopotamia.

About 2000 B.C. Egypt rose to new heights of power and wealth in the Middle Kingdom after a Dark Age of anarchy lasting a couple of centuries. A second Dark Age of foreign domination temporarily reduced her purchasing power from, say, 1700 to 1580 B.C. But after that date the Nile valley was reunified under Egyptian pharaohs who embarked on successful campaigns of conquest in Hither

Asia and annexed Palestine and Syria to their New Empire. As a result booty, in which subalterns and common soldiers shared, and tribute from defeated states swelled the national income and created on the Nile an unprecedented demand for imported goods. About the same time the kings of Ur between about 2000 and 1900 B.C. and then in 1790 B.C. Hammurabi unified Mesopotamia and made Ur and Babylon respectively imperial capitals, once more enriched by loot and tribute. And in the interval between the empires of Ur and Babylon an almost imperial status was attained by Mari on the Middle Euphrates, whence an easy caravan route leads across to the Levant coasts. Of course loot and conquest constitute no absolute increase in real wealth, but they do bring an absolute increase in purchasing power, since to the conquerors and plunderers the proceeds represent pure surplus.

It may well have been through exclusive access to the Egyptian and Mesopotamian markets thus constituted that the chieftains in Central Crete, mentioned already on p.115, had been able to raise themselves to kingly status. No doubt architectural features in their palaces at Knossos and Mallia, Phaestos and Hagia Triadha[94] seem more appropriate to a temple than to a residence, as if the kings were worshipped as gods or at least revered as the sole intermediaries between their followers and the divine powers. Yet under the ceremonial floors, magazines stocked with huge jars, once filled with wine or oil, and workshops are more reminiscent of the factories of merchant princes. Indeed by 1850 B.C. products from Cretan palace workshops were demonstrably being exported to Egypt and the Levant. The economic basis of a Minoan king's authority would then be a monopolistic grip on overseas trade with Egypt and Hither Asia. The profits of this trade were of course a share in the Oriental surplus. As such they not only served as capital for the expansion of specialized agriculture and the support of professionalized handicrafts. They would also render the profiteers independent of the gifts and offerings a barbarian chief traditionally receives from his followers.

In any case the Minoan kings were in command of an expendable surplus large enough to entice professional craftsmen – potters, fresco-painters, goldsmiths – from Egypt or Hither Asia to settle at their courts and by training Cretan apprentices to found Minoan schools of artist crafts-men. The immigrant masters and their disciples would have had a choice of patrons on the island; for, however uniform Middle Minoan civilization may appear, this archaeological uniformity apparently did not correspond to a political unity. Knossos may indeed have enjoyed a degree of hege-mony but, save between 1450 and 1400 B.C., was hardly the island's sole capital. And the Minoan 'priest-kings' proved exceptionally intelligent and appreciative patrons. The new class of specialist craftsmen in Crete displayed initiative and artistic sensibility lacking among their Oriental contem-poraries. This is most strikingly illustrated in the ceramic industry. In general wheel-made pots are aesthetically inferior to the hand-made vessels they superseded; they usually lack the grace of form and the variety of tasteful designs that give charm to the older, more individual pro-ducts. Professional potters in the Orient, if not evoked by the Urban Revolution, had been reduced by it to the lower classes. In fact most of the clientele came from the same classes, since rulers used vessels of metal or of stone. But in Crete the professional arrived as an honoured exponent of a new art and at a time when the new priest-kings were not yet too rich to use earthenware on their tables. So they did in fact produce delicate and lovely vases, fit to appear on a royal board. Indeed Middle Minoan pottery was so fine and so highly esteemed even in luxurious Egypt that a

Cretan vase was deemed worthy of inclusion among the treasures buried in the tomb of a high Egyptian noble.

What is so plain in the potters' craft could just as well be demonstrated in metal work and military equipment. Middle Minoan craftsmen developed in an original way the traditions of Oriental and Early Aegean armourers. I might mention long rapiers, represented by a royal weapon from the palace of Mallia that exceeds in length and finish the longest known from earlier Asiatic or Egyptian tombs. It is even possible that Minoan smiths invented the technique of core casting; spear-heads, provided with sockets by folding, were certainly replaced by ones with cast sockets, but the technique may have been invented and applied earlier in Syria and thence transmitted to Crete. To deal with the volume of secular business professional clerks were maintained in the palaces and they devised conventional systems of keeping records and accounts – at first hieroglyphic characters, and then a cursive script, 'linear A',[95] traced on clay.

The Minoan palaces were more than once destroyed, only to be rebuilt generally on a larger scale. Some of these catastrophes may be attributed to earthquakes, to which Crete is notoriously subject. But the destruction of Knossos about 1450 B.C. – at the end of Late Minoan I – seems to have involved a change of dynasty. The new rulers, who may have included the Minos of later Greek legend, introduced a new version of the Minoan cursive script – the so-called linear B – which was used also on the Greek Mainland at Mycenae, Pylos, and Thebes. They may have introduced a new language, Indo-European Greek. For the linear B texts have been read as a sort of archaic Greek,[96] though this decipherment is not universally accepted. Minos, if that were the new dynast's name, would then be an invader from Mainland Greece. In any case he seems to have established a sort of imperial rule over the rest of the island, supported perhaps by African mercenaries.[97] This 'empire' was short-lived. About 1400 B.C. the palace of Knossos was finally sacked and not rebuilt. The economic and political hegemony in the Aegean had passed to Mycenaean Greece.

There, it will be recalled (p. 115), warlike invaders, the 'Minyans', at the beginning of the Middle Helladic age about 1800 B.C., had laid waste and then reoccupied the Early Helladic townships. In the sequel local war-chiefs raised themselves to kingly rank; 'royal tombs' and frescoed palaces unmistakably exhibit contrasts between them and their retainers and subjects. Such kingship first emerged at Mycenae,[98] a point strategically situated to control a vital route from the southern Aegean to the Corinthian Gulf and so to the West and North. Two circles of shaft-graves represent the royal cemeteries perhaps of two parallel and contemporary royal houses. Both cemeteries were encircled by rings of upright slabs. Some at least of the shaft-graves were surmounted by sculptured stelae or gravestones depicting the king in a horse-driven chariot driving over a fallen foeman or hunting a lion. The tombs were crammed with bronze weapons, including enormous rapiers, ornaments, and vessels of precious metals, engraved gems, beads of semi-precious stones and amber, and wheel-made pots. Many of these objects were indubitably executed by Minoan artist-craftsmen, though these must sometimes have worked at Mycenae itself and not in Crete. It rather looks as if the wealth and economic power of the Shaft Grave kings were derived from successful raids on Cretan palaces;[99] some of their treasures would be loot, others the works of Minoan craftsmen, carried off captive or enticed away by the conquerors' booty. The Shaft Grave kings would thus have annexed by force and vio-

lence a fraction of the Oriental surplus, appropriated by
Minoan priest-kings.

The Shaft Grave cemeteries at Mycenae are believed to
have been in use from 1600 B.C. or a little earlier to at least
1450 B.C. But after 1500 began the erection of equally royal
tombs of a quite different kind – tholoi – at various sites in
the Peloponnese, Central Greece and Thessaly, and eventually at Mycenae itself. There the tholos tombs, nine in
number, might mark the accession of a new dynasty, oust-
ing the Shaft Grave lines just as the Pelopids replaced the
Perseids in Greek heroic tradition. Mycenaean tholoi are
spacious corbelled tombs, circular in plan, very neatly built,
either free-standing under a cairn or in an excavation in a
hillside from which only the apex would have projected
under a low artificial mound; in either case a passage,
walled but unroofed, gave access to the chamber.[37] Thus
these tholoi look like grand versions of the collective tombs
of the Western Mediterranean and Atlantic Europe, but in
contrast to the latter they never seem to have served as
family vaults but were used for the burial of a single
king[100] sometimes with his queen and one or two young
children. Commoners were buried in rock-cut chamber-
tombs that were genuine family vaults, used for successive
interments over several generations. Tholoi, when – exceptionally – found intact, were as royally furnished as the
earlier Shaft Graves. The furniture of the private rock-cut
tombs, though less spectacular, was also remarkably rich;
metal gear is plentiful though little gold or silver survives.
(The officiants at the later burials would perhaps have stolen
valuables accompanying the primary interments!)

Tholoi occur isolated or in small cemeteries – the nine at
Mycenae form the largest known group – and most at
sites that were the seats of legendary heroes. Many are
significantly located at the heads of southward-facing gulfs

– e.g. of the Gulf of Volo in Thessaly – or near ports on sea routes, as along the west coast of the Peloponnese. Thus their sites were peculiarly exposed to Minoan penetration but equally well-suited to form bases for sea raids on Crete. Tombs are our best guide to the extent of Mycenaean civilization. Domestic sites are less exhaustively known.

Mycenae[98] itself was hardly a city, but rather a strongly fortified citadel occupying only eleven acres and containing the royal palace and the dwellings of officials and retainers. Several villages, each with a cemetery of chamber-tombs, clustered round the citadel. True cities undoubtedly existed, but their sites, as at Argos and Thebes, are encumbered with classical and modern buildings, and their importance has to be inferred from the size of the associated cemeteries and a few accessible fragments of buildings, such as a palace at Thebes. While quite a number of citadels and a few open villages have been excavated or at least surveyed, nothing like a temple has come to light though temples are the most imposing and best known monuments of the historical period in Greece.

Mycenaean equipment, armament, and fashions of dress correspond so well with what Homer describes that the testimony of the Epics can profitably be used to supplement archaeological data on political and social conditions too. In the Iliad Greece is ruled by a number of 'god-born kings' (*diogenoi basilees*) – presumably the persons buried in tholoi. All acknowledge the overlordship of Agamemnon of Mycenae – archaeologically the richest centre in Bronze Age Greece – without being effectively subject to him; he is significantly styled 'king of men', never 'king of kings' as an Oriental monarch would have been. For all their claims to divine birth these 'kings' were not raised above society to anything like the height of an Oriental despot. Odysseus of Ithaka was indeed captain and helmsman of his vessel, but the crew were his 'companions', not serfs nor hired hands. According to their decipherers[101] the linear B texts mention two ranks below the king's: persons holding land from the king individually in return for military service ('barons') and villagers enjoying the usufruct of plots in communal land that were subject to redistribution. 'Barons' were undoubtedly buried in chamber tombs which contain plenty of appropriate weapons. Were villagers equally well buried?[102] No other class of commoners' graves has been recognized. Palmer[103] has argued that craftsmen belonged to this lowest rank, and in some texts they are allegedly mentioned as cultivators as if they were not full-time specialists. But we have cited on p. 114 Homeric passages implying the free mobility of craftsmen and incompatible with any suggestion that they were tied to the land, as peasants might have been. In fact the craftsman's position should have been at least as fortunate as in Early Aegean times.

The Urban Revolution in Greece and Crete had not created a single State capable of restricting the free movement of individuals. It had created a number of virtually independent kinglets, each rich enough to be a generous patron. And these, although 'god-born', were practical men, not only combatants in war but competent in peace to lend a hand at manual work like boat-building. Nor were kings the only potential clients of craftsmen. The furniture of the rock-cut tombs discloses a substantial and prosperous middle class whose members certainly did purchase craft products. Finally the large number of independent courts and towns, many within easy walking distance one from the other, might easily have engendered competition for the services of a skilled artisan. Stimulated by access to so many and such appreciative markets, Mycenaean craftsmen displayed the same sort of originality and inventiveness as

their Minoan ancestors. If aesthetically Mycenaean manufactures after 1400 B.C. are inferior to Minoan products of
earlier date, technical progress was unchecked.

The Mycenaeans and probably the Minoans too had
doubtless secured a share in the Orient's surplus partly by
sheer rapine. 'Sacker of cities' was an honorific title applied
to Homeric heroes. The *Iliad* mentions incidentally the
looting of coastal towns in Asia Minor. The *Odyssey*[104]
gives a circumstantial account of a viking raid on the
Egyptian delta, which though admittedly fictitious was
intended to be plausible; note that the booty aimed at consisted of foodstuffs and slaves, not treasure. Mercenary
service in the Egyptian, Mitannian, or Hittite armies might
also have drawn some Oriental wealth to Greece. But most
was secured by legitimate trade in the Early Aegean and
Minoan manner. Cyprus, the Copper Island, became a
Mycenaean colony along with Rhodes and other Aegean
islands. On the Levant coasts a trading post, first Minoan
(1500–1400 B.C.), then Mycenaean, was established at
Ugarit (Ras Shamra)[105], the best port for communications
with Mesopotamia. Some sort of colony seems to have
been planted at Colophon too. Enormous quantities of
Mycenaean vases were imported into Egypt, Palestine,
and Syria, especially between 1400 and 1300 B.C. Of course
they had not arrived empty, but filled with wines, oil, and
unguents. These containers are the only archaeological
documents of a very substantial trade in perishable organic
materials and manufactures. But Cretan textiles are mentioned in texts from Mari on the Euphrates as early as
1800 B.C. The vessels that carried these Minoan-Mycenaean
wares and the merchants who disposed of them on the
Oriental markets were themselves Mycenaean. So all the
profits from this commerce went to enrich the Mycenaean
economy and even to augment the food supply. For some

of the proceeds of commerce as well as of raiding must have been foodstuffs.

By no means all the wares carried in Mycenaean bottoms and sold by Mycenaean merchants in Oriental markets were the produce of Greece and Cyprus. The Mycenaeans surely imported from barbarian Europe raw materials, particularly tin, for re-exportation at a profit to the Orient and for their own domestic and armament industries. The provenance of tin cannot be determined. But even the Mycenaean Shaft Grave kings prized amber[37] for its magic virtue, and their superstitious greed for this fossil resin was inherited by Tholos kings and by prosperous retainers on the Mainland and in Crete too. Now amber, of course, came from the Baltic, but some seems to have arrived in the manufactured state and to have come indirectly through Britain. In two Shaft Graves at Mycenae and in a tholos on the west coast were found crescentic necklaces of amber beads with very curiously perforated spacers. Now crescentic necklaces of this type were very popular in the British Isles. Again a gold-bound amber disk from a tomb at Knossos in Crete can be matched by six similar disks from Wiltshire barrows. Both the necklaces and the disk may therefore be accepted as imports, made in Britain. On the other hand segmented beads of faience, certainly of East Mediterranean manufacture, have turned up in no less than thirty-five Bronze Age burials in Southern England,[106] while a grave, significantly located between the south coast of Cornwall and the celebrated tin deposits of Bodmin Moor, was furnished with a dagger made in Greece between 1300 and 1200 B.C.[107] As trade of some sort between the Aegean and Britain is thus documented both by imports and exports, it is safe to infer that the Mycenaeans were drawing on Cornish tin to help to supply their own and the Oriental demand for this rare and vital element, while they may have been getting supplies from Bohemia too.

Cornish tin may have reached the Aegean by western seaways as it did a thousand years later. Mycenaean commerce in the Mediterranean is abundantly documented as far west as Sicily.[37] Mycenaean vases and other manufactures reached South-east Sicily in quite large quantities between 1400 and 1300 B.C. Even more pottery, some as early as 1500 B.C., was received on Lipari in the Aeolian Islands together with faience beads. Lipari indeed seems to have served as a regular transhipment station in a commerce that was assuredly indirect. Its westward extension is harder to follow; only a Cypro-Mycenaean copper ingot from Sardinia and a couple of faience beads from South France, Almeria, and Brittany respectively positively attest connexions with the Aegean till we reach England. But some prehistorians would regard the cemeteries of Arles, Los Millares, and Alcalá (p. 117) as by-products of this prehistoric tin trade. On the other hand Cornish tin may have joined the well-attested stream of amber on the Saale and thence been transported across the Brenner Pass to be shipped down the Adriatic or to be carried across the Apennines along the familiar route via Bologna, Florence, Rome, and Naples for shipment to Lipari. In any case Minoan Crete and Mycenaean Greece did provide a reliable market for some products of barbarian Europe and, in so far as these were re-exported, increased their share in the Oriental surplus.

Thanks to their participation therein Aegean peoples had been enabled to build up an urban civilization without submitting to that extreme concentration of economic power that had been an inevitable condition for the Urban Revolution in Egypt and Mesopotamia, and without becoming subject to even economic domination by these totalitarian purchasers. Even in the Aegean the Urban

Revolution may have reduced the peasantry to a lower class of virtual serfs. No doubt a substantial proportion of the Oriental capital transferred to Crete and Greece, was concentrated in the hands of kings. But judging by the contents of private tombs, quite a generous share must have been dispersed through a broad middle-class of townsfolk and 'companions', not separated from the many kings by an impassable economic gulf. In particular the Revolution had left to craftsmen much the same kind of opportunities that they had enjoyed in Early Aegean times. In this sense Mycenaean society may be called already European.

Nevertheless this Late Aegean civilization collapsed. A disproportionate amount of its relatively small social surplus was absorbed by the armament industry. Too much real capital was squandered in destructive dynastic struggles of which the legendary Trojan War was just the culmination. Barbarian hordes, some at least exploited and trained by Mycenaeans, after annihilating Hittite civilization and ravaging the cities of the Levant, eventually finished off the Mycenaean civilization, rotten with internal contradictions. The half-legendary Dorian Invasion finally plunged the Aegean world into a Dark Age. But not before the Aegean surplus had served as the foundation for a bronze industry in Temperate Europe in which Aegean traditions of craftsmanship could still operate freely.

CHAPTER 10

THE ESTABLISHMENT OF A METALLURGICAL INDUSTRY IN TEMPERATE EUROPE

ARCHAEOLOGICAL books inevitably give the impression that it was the Mycenaeans' greed for amber that made it worthwhile to organize a hazardous traffic up unregulated rivers and across densely wooded mountains, beset with wild beasts and quarrelsome tribes, from Central Europe to the Aegean. This is, of course, less than half the truth. Amber is a readily identifiable substance of known provenance, so that its distribution by human agency can be precisely plotted on a map. No such precision is possible at present in the case of tin, copper, and gold, still less for salt and organic materials that have simply vanished. Archaeologists have learned a great deal about the routes and mechanisms of the prehistoric amber trade, but it must never be forgotten that other and more vital merchandise was associated with the amber.

Graves and hoards containing amber clearly mark the route by which the fossil resin travelled from the coasts of Jutland towards Greece.[37] All was carried up the Elbe as far as its junction with the Saale. Here there was a bifurcation. One route followed the Elbe into Bohemia, then crossed the Hercynian Forest to the Danube and went upstream to the mouth of the Inn. There it rejoined the alternative route up the Saale, down the Main, and across to the Danube. The combined streams went up the Inn to the Brenner Pass and then, after an easy porterage, down the Adige to vanish in the Adriatic, or, crossing the Apennines, to be shipped to the Aeolian Islands and so to Greece. Other commodities were certainly transported along the same route. Tin from Cornwall could have joined it on the Saale, since a contemporary trade route from the Channel coasts across Holland and North-west Germany is well documented. The tin deposits of Bohemia and Vogtland already lay close to the amber route itself. Sammland amber probably joined that from Jutland on the Saale. A traffic in Transylvanian gold, carried overland from Szeged to Budapest and thence paddled up the Danube to its confluence with the Inn, can reliably be inferred.

The commercial system thus disclosed had been called into being to supply the Aegean market; it was the accumulated resources of the Minoan-Mycenaean civilization that guaranteed to the distributors a livelihood, indeed an adequate recompense, for the hazards and hardships of their travels. But once established, the machinery could profitably be used to supply the demands for metal gear of barbarian societies living on or near its routes. These societies did in fact enter the Bronze Age, using metal regularly for weapons and ornaments, while the rest of Temperate Europe remained in the New Stone Age! The hoards that mark the Amber Route contain, besides amber, bronze weapons and ornaments certainly intended for local barbarian markets. The hoards are in fact generally considered to be the stock-in-trade of itinerant merchant-artificers who had been forced to bury their wares by some sudden danger. The itinerants carried of course amber and doubtless other goods destined for the civilian market, but also semi-manufactured bronze ware – dagger-blades, axe-heads, etc. – to be mounted and finished off to the order of a local barbarian purchaser.

A common constituent in many hoards all along the Amber Route from the North Sea to the Adriatic and also in Italy and as far east as Transylvania is a neck-ring or torque with recoiled ends. Such are believed to have served as the units or ingots in which copper was distributed and so have been nicknamed 'ingot torques'. Now just such ingot torques were current in the Levant round about 2000 B.C. There, too, they were offered in temples, presumably as units of value. At Ugarit[108] one is represented as worn by a deity who was apparently the patron of a craft-clan or guild of skilled metal-workers. Were the prospectors who had first located the ores of Central Europe and initiated their exploitation, immigrants from Syria? That seems highly probable, even if we admit that they could not profit from their discoveries till Minoan Crete and Mycenaean Greece offered a market for their winnings that was both reliable and accessible. Had they brought their 'guild organization' with them as well as their standard of value? If so, they must have admitted their European apprentices to membership of the clan. We shall see that metal-workers were not members of the local tribal societies among whom they worked and who are represented in the archaeological record by ceremonial burials.

In any case the distribution of ingot torques round the copper lodes of the Eastern Alps proves that exploitation had begun by 1500 B.C. Old opencast workings and adits, spoil heaps, furnaces, and other remains in the high alps above remote, thickly forested valleys give a vivid picture of an extractive industry estimated to have employed 500 workers.[109] But though certainly prehistoric, there is no conclusive evidence that these large-scale operations began before 1250 B.C. They may well have been preceded by working more accessible lodes or the alluvial ores such as are actually found in the tributaries of the Salzach to this day. In any case East Alpine, Slovakian, and other ores were being mined and smelted to supply the itinerant merchant-artificers actually engaged in the amber trade.

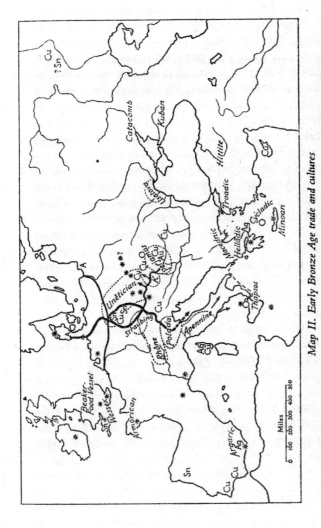

Map II. Early Bronze Age trade and cultures

A = Amber   Au = Gold   K = Kisapostag   Sn = Tin   —— = Mycenaean trade route

Ag = Silver   Cu = Copper   O = Obsidian   —— = Amber routes   * = Segmented fayence beads

In Central Europe and Italy the hoards in any one natural region are composed predominantly of local types of weapons and ornaments, and the same types are found in graves in an equally restricted province. These local peculiarities of metal types reflect the divergent tastes and fashions of distinct societies. For corresponding idiosyncrasies in pottery and burial distinguish the populations of each area. In Map II (p. 165) some of the more important cultures that represent these societies in the archaeological record have been indicated. Amber being a common factor in all these regional cultures, the transcontinental amber trade was no more a through traffic than the maritime trade discussed on p. 160. The agents would have confined their perambulations normally to one culture-province, that is, tribal territory, catering to local tastes, but exchanging at the tribal frontiers amber and other commodities destined for the Mycenaean market. In fact few hoards are composed exclusively of local types. The latter, though concentrated in graves and hoards in a single province, do occur sporadically far beyond its boundaries; for instance, Irish axes have been found in hoards in the Saale valley and in Sweden, Central German pins in England, Bohemian pins in Upper Italy and Switzerland.

In the Early Bronze Age peninsular Italy, Central Europe, the West Baltic coastlands, and the British Isles were united by a single system for the distribution of metalware, rooted in the Aegean market. To this economic unity corresponded no political or cultural unity. The distributive machinery served a number of archaeological cultures distinguished one from the other by divergences in pottery, dress, personal ornaments, burial rites, and even favourite types of dagger or axe. All were, of course, based on mixed farming. But in the Beaker and Wessex cultures of Britain, and in the still half-neolithic cultures of th'

North Sea coasts, Denmark, and South Sweden the chief emphasis was laid on pastoral pursuits. In both these areas and also in Brittany burial under barrows might denote a survival of Battle-axe traditions in ideology too. In Central Europe burial in flat graves was the rule in the Unětician culture of Moravia, Bohemia, and Central Germany as among numerous smaller groups, designated Straubing (Bavaria), Mad'arovce (Slovakia), Nagy Rév (Upper Tisza basin), Perjámos (Tisza-Maros region), Polada (Upper Italy) and others. But in the Kisapostag culture of Northwest Hungary the dead were cremated, the ashes inurned and then buried in cemeteries that may justly be termed urnfields just as in the Late Neolithic Baden culture of the same region.

In most cultures there is no explicit archaeological evidence for a concentration of political and economic power whether by chiefs or gods. But the Wessex barrows of England and the contemporary Armorican Bronze Age barrows in Brittany are so rare and rich that they might be attributed to an aristocracy of rich ranchers if only commoners' graves could be recognized. But it is only on the Saale and on the Warta that a few richly furnished burials under huge barrows are juxtaposed to cemeteries of normal Unětician flat graves and so reflect unambiguously a contrast between chiefs and followers or rather subjects. Perhaps these chiefs had been made economically independent of their fellow-tribesmen's customary gifts by generous presents and bribes from merchants who traversed their territories. But they founded no durable dynasties and their shortlived kingdoms were of a minute size. Though poorer than the Early Kuban chiefs (p. 137), they concentrated enough wealth to form stimulating markets and as patrons to encourage craftsmanship, but certainly not enough to promote unaided the mining developments in the Austrian

Alps, just mentioned on p. 164. The Wessex aristocracy devoted most of the surplus they annexed to the construction and embellishment of monumental sanctuaries like Stonehenge and Avebury. A vast amount of social labour is crystallized in their stones and ditches, but no expendable surplus; they could not fulfil the economic rôle played by the Sumerian temple.

On the other hand the peasant villages of Central Europe and Italy were now large enough and prosperous enough to constitute effective markets for craft products and metalwares once the initial difficulty of starting up the extractive and distributive industries had been overcome by the proximity of the Aegean market. Metal tools, though probably still too costly for use in clearing land, would yet indirectly augment the productivity of farming by facilitating the construction of ploughs and carts. The former were certainly in general use. In Upper Italy and in the Middle Danube basin in Hungary and Slovakia the sites of Early Bronze Age villages are marked by tells. So the rural economy was advanced enough to allow the continuous cultivation of the adjacent löss lands. Further north and west cemeteries of 250 or more graves point to some permanence of settlement. No village is likely to have been big enough and rich enough to support a resident smith save perhaps in Italy and Hungary; there a few moulds for casting Early Bronze Age types have been found in the tells. But even in Italy more such moulds have been found in caves that at all times offer convenient shelter to itinerants. Neither in Italy and Central Europe nor yet in the British Isles and Northern Europe are graves of smiths recognizable at this period. Hence peasant villages and pastoral groups most likely relied on itinerant artificers, carrying with them their simple tools, raw materials and half-finished products – in fact on the agents of the amber trade. Really most farmers were still content with a neolithic equipment; metal was used primarily for arms, personal ornaments, and craft-tools.

The life of the smiths and pedlars who manufactured and distributed these wares was doubtless hard and perilous. They were rewarded neither with great riches nor with a high rank in society. Judging by the evidence from Italy and later from England[110] their temporary abodes were natural caves rather than houses in the villages. As no smiths' graves have been recognized, they may have been left outside the social organization, presumably based on kinship, of the pastoral and agricultural communities whose cemeteries we know. Perhaps, as in Syria, metal workers in Europe were organized in a craft clan that gave them the support of a sort of intertribal trade union organization. Probably, too, each bore 'the mark of Cain' to announce: 'This stranger is not an enemy to be slain at sight but the bearer of things you want and knowledge useful for you'.[111] Since in barbarian societies security of the person is guaranteed by the blood feud alone, some such convention must be assumed. In any case despite all disabilities European metal-workers were free. They were not tied to any one patron or even to a single tribal society. They were producing for an intertribal, if not an international, market. And behind their immediate barbarian clients was Mycenae with its rich rewards and insatiable demands.

A market of this kind offered every inducement to originality on the part of the producers. At the same time their very itineracy and far-flung commercial contacts should fertilize native genius. They met on the frontiers of their territories colleagues working to satisfy the divergent tastes of other societies and perhaps employing ores or metal of different composition. Among the wares they handled they would see products of more distant schools of metal-work for comparison with familiar local types. Thus the peculiar structure of the European bronze industry induced an effective pooling of experiences, gained in different environments, and of traditions evoked by divergent popular tastes. As a result European bronze workers did display inventiveness and ingenuity to an exceptional degree. Their basic techniques such as the use of valve moulds and core-casting were indeed most probably inventions of the Orient. But their products – tools, weapons, toilet articles – underwent a rapid typological development to which the Ancient East offers no parallel. And here typological development means progressive and cumulative modification in the direction of higher efficiency. Thus in at most five centuries the flat celt or axe-head had been developed through flanged types and palstaves to the socketed celt that is just as efficient as the familiar shaft-hole axe (p. 30) but requires only half as much expensive metal.[112] In even less time the triangular knife-dagger developed through ogival dirks and rapiers into an effective and reliable cut-and-thrust sword. By 1300 B.C. the toggle pin of Hither Asia had been converted by two convergent routes into a brooch or safety-pin.

Of course progressive technology was not confined to the bronze industry, though best documented therein. We have for instance only badly dated fragments to illustrate comparable developments in the older craft of carpentry. The achievements of barbarian craftsmen in Temperate Europe can be inferred from the judgments of their civilized contemporaries in Greece and Crete. We have already seen (p. 159) that crescentic necklaces and a gold-bound disk of amber, reputedly made in Britain, found purchasers in the Aegean between 1600 and 1400 B.C. A century later the reputation of Continental smiths was so high that one of them found a patron at Mycenae itself. There has recently been found the stone valve-mould he used for casting axe-heads of a distinctively North Italian pattern. About the same time Continental European fashions in pins and perhaps also in dress and armament began to spread to Greece. But this may reflect an infiltration of barbarian chieftains and their retainers as much as an appreciation of barbarian skills by civilized townsfolk.

Of course the barbarians had learned their primary techniques from Asiatic or at least Aegean masters. But they had improved on them and applied them to new devices. So, too, the extractive and distributive industries that supplied them with materials had been developed in reliance on Oriental or at least Aegean markets. But barbarian farmers had grown prosperous enough to exert an effective demand and to sustain it when the Mycenaean market collapsed. The decisive rôle of the Aegean in the initial phase is conclusively demonstrated by the restricted distribution of Early Bronze Age culture, or to be precise, of graves furnished with metal gear of that type. These are found only along the Amber Route with its British and Transylvanian extensions, and, of course, in Sicily and South-east Spain. Meanwhile local societies made shift with a neolithic equipment, relieved by a few metal tools of archaic type, throughout France and most of the Iberian peninsula, in the coniferous zone of Northern Europe – and for some time even in the deciduous forests there, too – and in most of the Balkan peninsula and Eastern Europe. Only on the steppes between the Caucasus and the Urals was the metallurgical industry of the Kuban culture, already described on pp. 136-40, in effective operation. But there are no indications that at this time it affected developments in Central Europe or was affected thereby. It constituted an autonomous economic system supplying the Eastern Pontic tribes alone.

The Prehistory of European Society

In temperate Europe by 1500 B.C. had been established a distinctive politico-economic structure such as had existed a thousand years earlier in the Aegean, but nowhere else in the Bronze Age world. An international commercial system linked up a turbulent multitude of tiny political units. All these, whether city-states or tribes, while jealously guarding their autonomy, and at the same time seeking to subjugate one another, had none the less surrendered their economic independence by adopting for essential equipment materials that had to be imported. As an additional return for this sacrifice they also benefited from a free circulation of ideas and their exponents, while new opportunities for a livelihood were opened up to farmers' younger sons. Whoever had the perseverance to earn initiation into the appropriate mysteries of technique and the courage to face the enormous risks and severe hardships involved, could escape the necessity of growing his own food and shake off the bonds of allegiance to an overlord or the more rigid fetters of tribal custom.

The author has neither the space nor the knowledge at his disposal to show in detail how closely this Bronze Age system foreshadowed the peculiarities of European polity in Antiquity, the Middle Ages, and Modern Times. Obviously all the essential features outlined above were replicated in Classical Greece. Slavery and totalitarianism temporarily distorted the pattern within the Hellenistic monarchies and the Roman Empire. But barbarian Europe outside their frontiers was a direct continuation of Bronze Age Europe as just described. In the sequel centralized empires were never permanent enough, and seldom efficient enough, to root out fissiparous traditions of local autonomy. The national states that eventually emerged were indeed enormously larger than our Bronze Age tribes and fewer in number. But they have all shown themselves just as mutually jealous in policy and as competitive economically. All have been increasingly dependent on a supranational economic system for vital raw materials as well as for the disposal of their own products. While peasantries have often been reduced to serfdom even more rigorously than under the despotic monarchies of the Bronze Age Orient, craftsmen, the exponents of applied science, have preserved their traditional freedom of movement within a supranational economy. The metics at Athens, the wayfaring journeymen of the Middle Ages, and the migrant craft unionist 'of the nineteenth century are the lineal descendants of the itinerants just described. But so were the Natural Philosophers and Sophists in Classical Greece, the travelling scholars of medieval Europe, and the natural scientists who from the days of Galileo and Newton to 1945 freely exchanged information and ideas by publication, correspondence, and visits regardless of political frontiers.

BIBLIOGRAPHICAL NOTE

Most of the statements in the foregoing pages are supposed to be justified by archaeological facts and technical arguments set forth in tedious detail in the following of my books:

The Dawn of European Civilization (6th edition), London: Routledge and Kegan Paul, 1957 (cited *Dawn*).

New Light on the Most Ancient East (4th edition), London: Routledge and Kegan Paul, 1952 (cited *NLMAE*).

Piecing Together the Past, London: Routledge and Kegan Paul,
1956.

Social Evolution, London: Watts and Co., 1951.

For special points, not there documented or discussed, the notes often refer the reader to special books and articles in periodicals; for the latter the following abbreviations are used:

AJA.	*American Journal of Archaeology.*
Ant. J.	*Antiquaries' Journal*, Society of Antiquaries of London.
BPI.	*Bullettino di Paletnologia Italiana*, Rome.
Instarch AR.	University of London Institute of Archae-ology, *Annual Report.*
JRAI.	*Journal of the Royal Anthopological Institute*, London.
L'Anthr.	*L'Anthropologie*, Paris.
PPS.	*Proceedings of the Prehistoric Society*, Cambridge.
Proc. Soc. Ant. Scot.	*Proceedings of the Society of Antiquaries of Scot-land*, Edinburgh.
PZ.	*Praehistorische Zeitschrift*, Leipzig.
SA.	*Sovietskaya Arkheologiya*, Institut Istorii Materialnoi Kul'tury, Moscow-Leningrad.

NOTES

1. Archaeological terms, methods, and assumptions have been explained in greater detail in my book *Piecing Together the Past*.
2. The latest comprehensive account is given by F. E. Zeuner, *Dating the Past*, London, 1954.
3. See also Libby, *Radio-Carbon Dating*, Chicago, 1950.
4. I have examined the possibilities of drawing sociological inferences from archaeological data in *Social Evolution*.
5. *SA.*, I, 1936, 63.
6. Bittel, K., and Rieth, A., *Die Heuneburg an der oberen Donau: ein frühkeltischer Fürstensitz*, Stuttgart, 1951, 51.
7. This distinction has been best expounded by C. S. Coon in Chapple and Coon, *Principles of Anthropology*, London, 1947.
8. For instance Melanesian villages used to dispatch expeditions to quarry stone for axes.
9. Tolstov found that the skeletons in double graves in Khorasmia (south of the Aral Sea) had not been buried simultaneously; the grave had been reopened after an interval presumably when the second member of the couple met a natural death. *Instarch AR.*, XIII, 1957.
10. Garrod, D. A. E., ' The Mugharet el-Emireh in Lower Galilee: Type Station of the Emiran Industry', *JRAI.*, 85, 1955, 141-62.
11. Pradel, L., 'L'Abri Audi: pièces inédites et considérations générales', *L'Anthr.*, 56, 1952, 232-40.
12. The only general up-to-date account of fossil men is R. Grahmann, *Urgeschichte der Menschheit*, Stuttgart, 1952; American edition projected.
13. The best general account of palaeolithic cultures and art is Breuil and Lantier, *Les Hommes de la pierre ancienne*, Paris, 1951.
14. *Antiquity*, XXIV, 1950, 4-11; XXVIII, 4-14; XXX, 98-101; *SA.*, XXV, 1956, 13-34, 173-188; 285-296.
15. Prošek, 'Szeletien na Slovensku', *Slovenská Archeológia*, I, 1953, 133-94; Vértes, 'Neuere Ausgrabungen . . . in der Höhle von Istállóskö', *Acta Archaeologica Hungarica*, V, 1955, 125-287. On wider issues see also Freund, *Die Blattspitzen des Paläolithikums in Europa*, Bonn, 1952.
16. Childe, 'Kostienki', *Instarch AR.* XII, 1956, 8-19, and Russian literature there cited.

Notes

17. E. Saccasyn della Santa, *Les Figures humaines du Paléolithique*, Anvers, 1947.
18. *BPI.*, n.s. VIII, 1952, 3-18; *Rivista di Scienze preistoriche*, V, 1950, 1-48; VIII, 127-37; IX, 80-8.
19. Vaufrey, R., 'L'Art rupestre nord-africain', *Archives* de l'Institut de Paléontologie Humaine, Mém. 20, Paris, 1939.
20. Pericot, L., *Historia de España: Epocas primitiva y romana*, Barcelona, 2nd ed., 1942.
21. A summary account of European mesolithic cultures with references to original reports is given in my *Dawn*.
22. *L'Anthr.*, XLIX, 1939-40, 702; *Rivista di Studi Liguri*, XIV, 1948, 16-19.
23. A. Rust, *Das altsteinzeitliche Renntierjägerlager Meiendorf*, Neumünster, 1937; id. *Die alt- und mittelsteinzeitlichen Funde von Stellmoor*, Neumünster, 1943.
24. J. G. D. Clark, *Star Carr*, Cambridge, 1954.
25. The fishing tackle and its survivals are specially well described by J. G. D. Clark in *Prehistoric Europe: the Economic Basis*, London, 1952.
26. *Suomen Museo*, LVI, Helsinki, 1949, 1-26.
27. To use the terminology of Lewis H. Morgan, *Ancient Society*, New York, 1871, with the modification I proposed in *Social Evolution*.
28. As explained in more detail in my *Man Makes Himself* (Watts and Co.).
29. H. Helbaek, 'Archaeology and Agricultural Botany', *Instarch AR.*, IX, 1953, 44-59.
30. Recent zoological text-books, all German, are discordant; latest summary in 36 *Berichte d. röm.-germ. Komm.*, Deutsches Arch. Inst., Frankfurt, 1955, 1-50.
31. This determination has been made by Prof. Zeuner since the publication of his date for Jericho II in *Antiquity*, XXX, 1956.
32. K. Kenyon, *Antiquity*, XXX; *Palestine Exploration Quarterly*, 1956, 1-16.
33. R. Braidwood, *The Near East and the Foundations of Civilization*, (Eugene, Oregon), 1952; *Sumer*, VII, Baghdad, 1952, 102-10: *Antiquity*, XXIV, 1950, 190-6.
34. C. S. Coon, 'Cave Explorations in Iran', *University of Pennsylvania Museum Monographs*, Philadelphia, 1951.
35. Fairservis, 'Excavations in the Quetta Valley', *Anthrop. Pubs. Amer. Mus. Nat. Hist.*, 45, ii, New York, 1956.

Notes

36. Childe, *NLMAE* – a general source for all early cultures in the Near East not otherwise documented.
37. For further details and references to original sources see my *Dawn*.
38. A. Steensberg, 'With Crackling Flames', *Kuml*, Aarhus, 1955, gives a convenient account of systems of cultivation based on clearance of forest by fire.
39. At Karanovo in Bulgaria; verbal information from V. Mikov.
40. The 'Cardial' colonists might have been reinforced by other immigrants from Africa with a culture parallel to the Almerian, described in section iv.
41. In a test pit at Otzaki sherds decorated with cardium impressions occûrred in the layer below that yielding unpainted Starčevo ware, Milojčić in *Jahrbuch d. deutsch. Arch. Inst.*, LXIX, *Arch. Anzeiger*, 1954, 11–23.
42. Vaufrey, *La Préhistoire de l'Afrique*, 1: *Maghreb*, Paris, 1955.
43. The only general account of the African monuments remains Frobenius, L., 'Der kleinafrikanische Grabbau', *PZ.* viii, 1916, 1–84.
44. Emery, W. B., 'An Egyptian Queen's Tomb of 5000 Years Ago', *Illus. London News*, 2 June 1956, 646–8.
45. The term was coined by Piggott, who explains the concept in *The Neolithic Cultures of the British Isles*, Cambridge, 1954.
46. F. Hančar, *Das Pferd in prähistorischer ... Zeit*, Vienna, 1955 (*Wiener Beiträge zur Kulturgeschichte*, XI), gives a particularly good German account of the whole rural economy of Tripolye, but he accepts Russian guesses at absolute dates that are higher than those accepted for other provinces in his own book and in this.
47. Krichevskii, *SA.* vi, 1940.
48. *The Neolithic Cultures of the British Isles;* an alternative view on which some at least of the colonists would have arrived by sea on the west coasts – ultimately presumably from the Iberian Peninsula – once favoured by the present writer, has been restated with fresh evidence by Case, *Ant. J.*, XXXVI, London, 1956, 11–30.
49. The probability that the Windmill Hill culture is not Western, in the sense of derived from South France, but rather Northern and sprung from the same source as the First Northern culture that is best known in Denmark is envisaged by Piggott in *PPS.*, XXI, 1955.
50. *Wiadomosci Archeol.*, XVII, 1950.

Notes

51. Cf. Clark in *Prehistoric Europe*.
52. *Suomen Museo*, LVI, 1949, 2-7.
53. Hančar, *Das Pferd*, gives a good summary of the voluminous literature without, however, mentioning the evidence cited in n. 52.
54. For further details and all archaeological evidence for which no other reference is given see my *NLMAE*, 1952.
55. Moret, *From Tribe to Empire*, and *The Nile and Egyptian Civilization*, London, 1926 and 1927.
56. Narmer is depicted twice on his palette wearing the crown of either Upper or Lower Egypt, but not both at once; he had a tomb at Abydos, smaller and less elaborate than those of Aha and his successors, but none at Saqqara. So I now think that the final unification, attributed by the Greeks to Mena (Menes) was accomplished by Aha; so Emery, *Hor-Aha* (*Excavations at Saqqara*, 1937-8), Cairo, 1939. Cf. also *Great Tombs of the First Dynasty*, II, London, 1954.
57. This has not been observed by excavators, but can be inferred from the disposition of the attendants' graves at Abydos in the light of Emery's observations at Saqqara in 1956. Emery, *Illus. London News*, 2 June 1956.
58. Length and breadth observed, height inferred in mastaba of Queen Her-neit by Emery, 1956.
59. At Tarkhan and Ezbet el-Wâlda near Helwan.
60. A. Schneider, *Die sumerische Tempelstadt*, Essen, 1920.
61. H. Frankfort, *The Birth of Civilization in the Near East*, London, 1951.
62. Deimel, 'Sumerische Tempelwirtschaft zur Zeit Urukaginas und seiner unmittelbaren Vorgänger', *Analecta Orientalia*, II, Rome, 1931, where 'Urukagina's Reform Decree' is translated.
63. Jacobsen, 'Primitive Democracy in Ancient Mesopotamia', *J. Near Eastern Studies*, II, Chicago, 1943, 159-72.
64. Jacobsen, 'The Sumerian King-List', *Assyriological Studies*, II, Oriental Institute, University of Chicago, 1939.
65. E.g. by E. Heinrich, 'Schilf und Lehm', *Studien z. Bauforschung*, Heft. 6, Berlin, 1934.
66. On the rôle of the State in the Bronze Age Orient see F. M. Heichelheim, *Wirtschaftsgeschichte des Altertums*, Leyden, 1938,
67. For instance in the so-called Cappadocian tablets, the correspondence of a colony of Assyrian merchants established at Kanesh (Kul-tepe) on the plateau of Anatolia about 1850 B.C.

Notes

68. Usually termed 'The Praise of Writing' and purporting to be the letter written by a father to encourage his son in his studies by contrasting most unfavourably the professions of farmer and craftsmen with that of the clerk. Translation in Moret, *op. cit.*, and often.

69. Lefebvre, *Le Tombeau de Pétosiris*, Cairo, 1923-4; the artist may have copied the metal-workers from a much older tomb picture though faithfully reproducing the costumes and vessels of his own time. Cf. *JRAI.*, LXXIV, 1494, 21.

70. For Cyprus the best summary is by J. R. Stewart, in *Handbook to the Nicholson Museum*, Sydney, 1948.

71. *Archaeologia*, LXXXVIII, 1938, pls. VII-IX.

72. Xanthudides in *Essays in Aegean Archaeology presented to Sir Arthur Evans* (ed. Casson, Oxford, 1927).

73. So Davies' report (*J. Hellenic Studies*, XLIX, 1929, 93-4) must be due to a misapprehension.

74. Evans, *The Palace of Minos*, I (1921), 23.

75. L. Bernabò Brea in *PPS.*, XXI, 1955, 144 ff.

76. Cf. my *Social Evolution*, p. 56 ff.

77. Cf. G. Glotz, *Ancient Greece at Work*, London, 1926.

78. Described in a late Latin poem, *Ora Maritima*, by Avienus; cf. C. F. C. Hawkes in *Ampurias*, XIV, 1952.

79. Fully described by Piggott, *Neolithic Cultures of the British Isles*.

80. Childe, *Ant. J.*, XXII, 1942.

81. *Vita Sancti Columbae*, Book. II, chap. 43.

82. John Morris, 'Celtic Saints', *Past and Present*, No. 11 (April 1957), 2-16.

83. On this culture see also Bailloud, G., and Mieg de Boofzheim, P., *Les Civilisations néolithiques de la France*, Paris, 1955.

84. 'Indogermanskskii Vopros archeologicheski razreshennyi', in *Izvestia* Gos. Akademiya Istorii Material'noi Kul'tury, 100 ('Marr Festschrift'), Moscow-Leningrad, 1933, 158 ff.

85. Despite exaggerated claims made in America for this group of swineherds, their real significance is much too doubtful to warrant discussion in a book like this.

86. Childe, *Skara Brae*, London, 1931: Childe and Grant, 'Excavations at Rinyo, Rousay', *Proc. Soc. Ant. Scot.*, LXXIII, 1939; LXXXI, 1947.

87. Mongait, A. A., *Arkheologiya v S.S.S.R.*, Moscow, 1955, 124.

88. Moulds for casting axe-adzes and transverse axes of the types found at Maikop have turned up at Tepe Hissar near Damghan

Notes

on the plateau and at Shah Tepe on the Turkoman Steppe below it and are now in the University Museum, Philadelphia, and in Statens Historiska Museet, Stockholm, respectively.

89. Cf. e.g. Andrae, *Das wiedererstandene Assur*, 1938, p. 79 and fig. 39.

90. Angell, in Dikaios, *Khirokitia* (London, 1953) and Senyürek in *Belleten*, Türk Tarih Kurumu, 60, Ankara, 1951, 440–2.

91. Shaft graves in both areas, stelae and rings of uprights at Mycenae and on the steppes, hammer pins at Lerna in Greece, and Alaca Höyük.

92. Flint weapons were mounted in the same curious way by the Predynastic Amratians.

93. The transformation was accomplished by later invaders of the Saale–Warta culture from Central Europe.

94. For the Minoan civilization see Pendlebury, *The Archaeology of Crete*, London, 1939.

95. Tentatively read in 1957 as a Semitic dialect from the shores of the East Mediterranean by C. H. Gordon, *Antiquity*, XXXI, 1957, 124–30.

96. Ventris and Chadwick, *Documents in Mycenaean Greek*, Cambridge, 1956.

97. Evans, *The Palace of Minos at Knossos*, IV, (London, 1935), 887, suggests these were used to establish a sort of empire on the Greek Mainland.

98. For archaeological finds at Mycenae see G. Mylonas, *Ancient Mycenae: the Capital City of Agamemnon*, London, 1957, unless other reference be given.

99. So, for instance, Lorimer, *Homer and the Monuments*, London, 1950, 19, but compare Arne Furumark 'The Settlement at Ialysus and Aegean History', *Opuscula Archaeologica*, VI, Lund, 1950.

100. A. W. Persson, *The Royal Tombs at Dendra* (*Skrifter*, K. Human. Vetenskapssamfundet i Lund, xv), 1931, but see also Marinatos in *Illustrated London News*, 6 April 1957 for a tholos near Pylos containing at least six burials, amber beads, and traces of a hearse, and dated 1500 to 1425 B.C.

101. Ventris and Chadwick, as note 96, p. 123.

102. Two normal rock-cut tombs were found associated with one excavated village (Blegen, *Zygouries*, 1928), only children's graves at two others (Blegen, *Korakou*, 1921; Goldmann, *Excavations at Eutresis*, 1931)

103. *Achaeans and Indo-Europeans*, Oxford, 1956.

104. XIV, 246 ff.

105. C. F. A. Schaeffer, *Ugaritica*, I, Paris, 1939.

106. J. F. S. Stone and L. C. Thomas, *PPS.* XXII, 1956, 60.

107. Childe, *PPS.*, XVII, 1951, 95.

108. C. F. A. Schaeffer, *Ugaritica*, II, Paris, 1949, 'Porteurs de torques'.

109. Pittioni, 'Prehistoric Copper-mining in Austria', *Instarch AR.*, VII, 1951, 16–43.

110. I refer to the Late Bronze Age occupation of Heathery Burn cave, Co. Durham.

111. E. Herzfeld, *Iran in the Ancient East*, Oxford, 1941, 158 ff., suggested that this protective 'tribal mark' would have been borne by a 'race' of 'Prospectors' – perhaps our plano-occipital steep-heads – who diffused metallurgical knowledge in Europe and Asia; at least our Beaker-folk should have belonged to the tribe.

112. V. G. Childe, 'The Socketed Celt in Upper Eurasia', *Instarch AR.*, X, 1954, 11–25.

GLOSSARY-INDEX